SHIPS OF THE ROYAL NAVY

SHIPS OF THE ROYAL NAVY

by Raymond V B Blackman, MBE, CEng, FIMarE, FRINA
Editor of *Jane's Fighting Ships* 1949–50 to 1972–73

MACDONALD and JANE'S

First published 1973
Reprinted 1974
ISBN 0356 04596 X

Copyright © Raymond V B Blackman 1973

Published by Macdonald and Jane's (Macdonald and Company (Publishers) Ltd)
St Giles House, 49/50 Poland Street, London W1A 2LG

FOREWORD

This comprehensive handbook covers all the ships of the Royal Navy from major fighting ships on ocean deployment at the head, carriers and amphibious ships, deterrent and other nuclear powered submarines, descending through the backbone of the Fleet in the shape of highly specialized guided missile ships, the workhorses comprising the fast frigates now filling the role of the erstwhile standard destroyers, and the support ships without which a modern navy cannot function, down to the running feet constituted by the smaller craft employed on coastal duties, experimental ships and the auxiliaries of the fleet train.

A description of each class is given together with notes on the variations in individual ships and all the particulars of displacement and dimensions, armament and propelling machinery, as well as builders, keel-laying, launching and completion dates, and pennant numbers.

The manual might be said to offer a new presentation of the now almost entirely post-war designed Royal Navy, for there has been a complete turnover from old to new conceptions and it will be seen from a perusal of the pages that scarcely a ship of pre-war construction remains. There are one or two notable exceptions. HMS *Belfast,* for instance, is given a place of pride, *pour memoire,* with the major warships, for she was the largest cruiser in the Royal Navy and she is there, in perpetuity it is planned, for all to see in the London River; the last representative of the gun era, a memento of the past, but still wearing the White Ensign. Two others are the parent ships for submarines, HMS *Defiance* (ex-*Forth*), still serving in several capacities at Devonport, and HMS *Maidstone,* on military duties at Belfast.

But 99 per cent of the ships specified and pictured in the following pages reflect the drastic change which has taken place in naval architecture, marine engineering and scientific technology since the Second World War. Naval artillery has given way to guided missile systems and conventional torpedo mountings have been replaced by sophisticated rocketry giving a more positive and homing result. Radio has almost entirely supplanted visual means of signal communications, and radar has taken over all forms of search, target acquisition and fire control. Computers have relieved personnel of the tedious calculations necessary to point and prepare a ship's intricate equipment for action. The triple expansion steam reciprocating engine has almost entirely disappeared, and even the ultra-modern steam turbine and the super-charged diesel engine are giving way to the gas turbine, while nuclear reactors have become the prime motive in deterrent and fleet submarines. The habitability of warships has improved so much that accommodation for officers and ratings is now a first consideration in ships under construction instead of as formerly when it was contrived after the requirements of armament and machinery had been met.

When the oldest ships in this volume were originally built most contemporary vessels were still fought with the Mark 1 sight (the human eye), the Mark 1 computer (the human brain) and the Mark 1 manipulator (the human hand), but in the modern warships there are electronic eyes, mechanical brains and automatic hands.

Ships were formerly run by specialist gunnery and torpedo officers and salt-horse seamen still largely domestically used even to the extent of holystoning wooden decks (a vestige of the latter still remains in a few ships); but today the ships are managed and operated by a variety of officer scientists and weapon, electrical and mechanical engineers (many with university degrees) and senior rating diagnosticians and technicians educated to a high standard, while with steel decks and automatic appliances menial chores for junior ratings have largely disappeared.

Now that a modern warship is hardly less than a highly mobile black box with all action controlled by electronics and automation, it is becoming increasingly obvious that one well-placed hit could put

FOREWORD

her out of action almost completely, as she could hardly revert to being worked and fought by hand. So the ship that strikes first could be the winner by instant knock-out. It follows that the most efficient navy, and not necessarily the strongest, could be the winner too.

The Royal Navy is no longer the largest navy in the world. It was overtaken by the United States Navy, with far greater resources, during the Second World War; and since then the Soviet Navy has overtaken the Royal Navy too, by sheer weight of numbers. At present even France and China are contending for third place.

But the true measure of a navy is in the quality of its ships, the responsibility of the Controller of the Navy, and the calibre of its personnel. The former relies on the design inventiveness of the Royal Corps of Naval Constructors and the manual skill of the shipbuilders, while the latter depends on the training and the *esprit de corps* of the officers and ratings, the whole adding up to preparedness. The navy which is the best prepared is the navy that will be victorious.

While the Royal Navy is not the largest navy in the world, this author believes that it may well be the most soundly trained, both at sea and on shore.

The sea training is the direct responsibility of the Flag Officer Sea Training at Portland and eventually of the Commander-in-Chief, Fleet at his Northwood Headquarters (HMS *Warrior*), while shore training is under the Director-General of Naval Manpower and Training, Navy Department, Ministry of Defence, with establishments under the Commander-in-Chief, Naval Home Command at Portsmouth (HMS *Victory*). The Second Sea Lord and Chief of Naval Personnel is responsible for all training.

Colleges include the Royal Naval College, Greenwich; the Britannia Royal Naval College, Dartmouth (HMS *Dartmouth*); and the Royal Naval Engineering College, Manadon (HMS *Thunderer*); and the various modern technical schools include HMS *Caledonia* (Engineering), HMS *Collingwood* (Weapon and Electrical), HMS *Dolphin* (Submarine), HMS *Dryad* (Navigation and Direction), HMS *Excellent* (Gunnery), HMS *Fisgard* (Apprentices), HMS *Mercury* (Signal), HMS *Neptune* (Polaris), HMS *Sultan* (Marine Engineering), HMS *Vernon* (Torpedo and Anti-Submarine) and HMS *Vulcan* (Nuclear Propulsion): 'stone frigates' in which most naval personnel serve from time to time.

Criticism is frequently levelled at the number of naval officers and ratings on shore compared with those in ships, but it is the sound training inculcated at the naval colleges and schools which turns on the Ships of the Royal Navy and makes them tick.

Raymond Blackman

Portsmouth, 1973

PREFACE TO REPRINT

This book sold so well that only a few months after publication it was out of print. In making preparations for a reprint the opportunity was taken to update 17 pages, slipping in new names (*Spartan* for the eleventh nuclear powered fleet submarine, *Kingfisher, Cygnet, Petrel* and *Sandpiper* for the new 'Bird' class patrol craft, and *Black Rover* for the new fleet oiler); and to insert three more modern plates (a new illustration of the through-deck cruiser or light aircraft carrier *Invincible* under construction, a photograph of the guided missile armed destroyer *Norfolk*, first with the new 'Exocet' ship-against-ship launcher, and a photograph of HMS *Amazon*, the first of the new 'Type 21' patrol frigates, as completed).

Portsmouth, 1974

Raymond Blackman

CONTENTS

The five ships featured in BBC TV's 'At Sea with the Navy' programme.
Left to right *HMS Galatea, RFA Olmeda, HMS ARK Royal, RFA Regent, HMS Euryalus*

ARK ROYAL

Originally designated *Irresistible,* but launched as *Ark Royal,* this ship was the first British aircraft carrier to have a deck-edge lift, steam catapults built in as opposed to fitted later, and an 'interim' angled deck at $5\frac{1}{2}$ degrees to the centre line. The deck-edge lift was removed in 1959. The ship was originally armed with sixteen 4.5-inch guns, but four were suppressed in 1956, four in 1959, four in 1964 and four in 1969. *Ark Royal* was 'specially refitted' and modernized during March 1967 to February 1970.

Deck letter	R
Pennant no.	R 09
Displacement	43 060 tons standard, 50 786 tons full load
Dimensions	845 × 166 × 36 feet
Guided weapons	Four quadruple 'Seacat' missile launchers (fitted for)
Aircraft	30 fixed-wing plus 6 helicopters
Catapults	2 improved steam
Machinery	Parsons single reduction geared turbines, 4 shafts, shp : 152 000 = 31.5 knots
Boilers	8 Admiralty three-drum type
Complement	260 officers (as flagship)
	2 380 ratings (with Air Staff)
	2 640 maximum accommodation
Builders	Cammell Laird & Co. Ltd, Birkenhead
Laid down	3 May 1943
Launched	3 May 1950
Completed	25 Feb. 1955
Reconstructed	HM Dockyard, Devonport, 1967–1970

Modernization: The three-year special refit and rehabilitation *inter alia* enable her to operate both *Phantom* and *Buccaneer* Mark 2 jet aircraft. A fully angled deck, $8\frac{1}{2}$ degrees off the centre line of the ship, was fitted, involving two large extensions to the flight deck; and the size of the 'island' superstructure was increased. A new waist catapult with an increased launching speed allowed her to operate aircraft at almost 'nil' wind conditions; and a new direct acting gear was installed to enable larger aircraft to be landed on at higher speeds. Trials at sea with the 'Jump jet' *Harrier* V/STOL (vertical or short take-off and landing) aircraft have been carried out in *Ark Royal* since May 1971.

ARK ROYAL

Official

EAGLE

This ship was to have been named *Audacious,* but she was launched as *Eagle.* She was originally a sister ship of *Ark Royal.* As rebuilt she represented the zenith of British aircraft carrier construction. She incorporated the latest developments, and with an 8½ degree angled deck and advanced 984 radar she was one of the best equipped aircraft carriers in the world. She was fitted with a built-in improved pre-wetting system to counteract contamination in the event of radio-active fall-out or chemical hazard. Her damage control arrangements were exceptionally complete. The particulars given below applied before she de-commissioned. *Harrier* vertical or short take-off and landing aircraft touched down on and took off from *Eagle* in March 1970 *et seq.*

Deck letter	E
Pennant no.	R 05
Displacement	43 000 tons standard, 50 536 tons full load
Dimensions	811¾ × 171 × 36 feet
Guns	Eight 4.5-inch dual purpose
Guided weapons	Six quadruple 'Seacat' missile launchers
Aircraft	34 plus 10 helicopters
Catapults	2 steam
Machinery	Parsons single reduction geared turbines, 4 shafts, shp : 152 000 = 31.5 knots
Boilers	8 Admiralty 3-drum type
Complement	1 745 officers and ratings including ship's air staff but excluding complements of embarked air squadrons. 2 750 maximum accommodation
Builders	Harland & Wolff Ltd, Belfast
Laid down	24 Oct. 1942
Launched	19 Mar. 1946
Completed	1 Oct. 1951
Reconstructed	HM Dockyard, Devonport, 1959–1964

Reconstruction: The 4½-year rebuilding included the fitting of a full angled flight deck and new flight deck armour, the installation of two steam instead of hydraulic catapults for launching the latest naval aircraft, the erection of superstructure half as long again as the former 'island', and the incorporation of the most up-to-date living accommodation.
Disposal: HMS *Eagle* was de-stored in 1972 to await decision as to her disposal. Still at Devonport in 1974.
Cancellations: Two more front-line fixed-wing strike aircraft carriers of this type, *Africa* and the original *Eagle* of the class, and three much larger fleet attack aircraft carriers to have been named *Gibraltar, Malta* and *New Zealand,* were cancelled at the end of the Second World War.

EAGLE

HERMES

Originally a sister aircraft carrier, and the name ship, of a class including *Albion, Bulwark* and *Centaur,* but her design was so radically modified and improved that she was virtually of a different type, incorporating new equipment and advanced arrangements, including five post-war developments, namely the angled deck, steam catapults, deck landing sights, three-dimensional radar and deck-edge lift. The flight deck is angled $6\frac{1}{2}$ degrees off the axis of the hull, the biggest angle that could be practically contrived in an aircraft carrier of her size. The name originally assigned to the ship when projected was *Elephant.* Of the other four aircraft carriers of this class originally ordered, *Arrogant,* original *Hermes, Monmouth* and *Polyphemus* were cancelled in 1945. The aircraft carrier *Centaur* left Devonport to be scrapped in October 1972 and the larger aircraft carrier *Victorious* left Portsmouth in July 1969 to be broken up at Faslane.

Deck letter	H
Pennant no.	R 12
Displacement	23 900 tons standard, 28 700 tons full load
Dimensions	$744\frac{1}{4} \times 160 \times 29$ feet
Guided weapons	Two quadruple 'Seacat' missile launchers
Aircraft	12 plus 8 helicopters
Machinery	Parsons geared turbines, 2 shafts, shp : 76 000 = 28 knots
Boilers	4 Admiralty 3-drum type
Complement	1 834
	2 100 with air squadrons embarked
Builders	Vickers-Armstrongs Ltd, Barrow-in-Furness
Laid down	21 June 1944
Launched	16 Feb. 1953
Completed	18 Nov. 1959
Refitted	1964–1966
Converted	1 Mar. 1971 to 17 Aug. 1973 at HM Dockyard, Devonport

Conversion: The main features of the conversion of HMS *Hermes* to the commando ship role included the removal of the steam catapults and arrester gear ; the rearrangement of the interior to provide accommodation for the Royal Marine battalion with storage for its guns, ammunition, vehicles and communications ; changes to the radar equipment to meet the new purpose ; the installation of additional air-conditioning, larger diesel generators, new auxiliary boilers and evaporators for making fresh water ; the extension of automatic control of machinery ; and the modernization of the galley, bakery, laundry and storage facilities. The ship will still be able to operate fixed-wing aircraft not requiring arrester gear and catapults such as the *Gannet,* especially as her flight deck had already been strengthened to take *Harrier* V/STOL aircraft. The ship was recommissioned on 18 August 1973.

HERMES

ALBION   BULWARK

These ships were formerly fixed-wing aircraft carriers, and sister ships of *Centaur*, but were converted into commando ships, and are essentially hybrid helicopter carriers and fast troop transports. They can each carry a full commando, or battalion of Royal Marines, which the ships can quickly transport and land, complete with equipment, wherever required, and their helicopters are also able to disembark the commando's vehicles. During conversion some of the anti-aircraft guns were removed to provide space for the landing craft carried at built-in gantries in davit positions.

Deck letter	A and B, respectively
Pennant no.	R 07 and R 08, respectively
Displacement	23 300 tons standard, 27 705 tons full load
Dimensions	$737\frac{3}{4} \times 123\frac{1}{2} \times 28$ feet
Guns	Eight 40-mm. anti-aircraft
Aircraft	16 helicopters
Landing craft	4 LCVP
Machinery	Parsons geared turbines, 2 shafts, shp: 78 000 = 28 knots
Boilers	4 Admiralty 3-drum type
Complement	1 035 plus 733 Royal Marine Commando and troops
	900 in Bulwark
	Total accommodation for 1 923 to 1 937 officers and men

	Builders	Laid down	Launched	Completed	Converted
Albion	Swan Hunter & Wigham Richardson, Ltd, Tyne	23 Mar. 1944	6 May 1947	26 May 1954	1961–1962
Bulwark	Harland & Wolff, Ltd, Belfast	10 May 1945	22 June 1948	4 Nov. 1954	1959–1960

Although *Albion* was converted from a fixed wing aircraft carrier into a commando carrier two years later than *Bulwark* and embodied a number of improvements enabling her to carry *Wessex* helicopters and a larger military force it was *Albion* which was chosen to be de-commissioned on 1 March 1973 so that the required manpower and other commando resources could be diverted to *Hermes* being converted into a combined aircraft/commando carrier. *Albion* was towed from Portsmouth to the Clyde on 22 October 1973 for disposal.

BULWARK *Official*

RENOWN   REPULSE   RESOLUTION   REVENGE

In February 1963 it was officially stated that it was intended to order four or five 7 000-ton nuclear powered submarines each to carry 16 'Polaris' missiles, and it was planned that the first would be on patrol in 1968. Their hulls and machinery would be of British design. Four were ordered on 8 May 1963 (officially announced). The intention to build a fifth Polaris submarine was confirmed by the then Ministry of Defence on 26 February 1964, but this intention was rescinded by a new Minister of Defence on 15 February 1965. Each submarine is manned on a two-crew basis in order to get maximum operational time at sea. One complete crew relieves the other at approximately three-month intervals.

Displacement	7 000 tons standard, 7 500 tons surface, 8 400 tons submerged
Dimensions	425 × 33 × 30 feet
Guided weapons	16 'Polaris' tubes amidships for A-3 model missiles with a range of 2 875 miles
Tubes	Six 21-inch
Machinery	1 pressurized water-cooled nuclear reactor
	Geared steam turbines, 1 shaft, speed = 20 knots surface, 25 knots submerged
Complement	141 (accommodation for 154). Two crews

	No.	Builders	Laid down	Launched	Accepted
Renown	S 26	Cammell, Laird & Co. Ltd, Birkenhead	25 June 1964	25 Feb. 1967	Feb. 1969
Repulse	S 23	Vickers-Armstrongs, Ltd, Barrow-in-Furness	12 Mar. 1965	4 Nov. 1967	Oct. 1968
Resolution	S 22	Vickers-Armstrongs, Ltd, Barrow-in-Furness	26 Feb. 1964	15 Sep. 1966	Oct. 1967
Revenge	S 27	Cammell, Laird & Co. Ltd, Birkenhead	19 May 1965	15 Mar. 1968	Dec. 1969

RESOLUTION

Official

SCEPTRE   SOVEREIGN   SPARTAN   SUPERB   SWIFTSURE

HMS *Swiftsure* is the first vessel, and name-ship, of a new class of fleet or hunter-killer submarines powered by nuclear reactors. With her sister ships *Sovereign,* launched, *Superb,* laid down, and *Sceptre,* ordered, she is becoming known as the prototype of the 'S' class, which is the fourth distinctive class of nuclear powered conventionally armed submarines. (The first was HMS *Dreadnought,* the second class comprised the *Valiant* and *Warspite,* the third was the 'C' class, namely *Churchill, Conqueror* and *Courageous,* and the fifth will be the SSN 11 (building number) at present unnamed, *et seq.* The order for the seventh nuclear powered fleet submarine, of 'improved' type (*Swiftsure*), was in the 1967–68 Estimates, for the eighth (*Sovereign*) in the 1968–69 Estimates, for the ninth (*Superb*) in the 1970–71 Estimates, for the tenth (*Sceptre*) in the 1971–72 Estimates and for the eleventh (*Spartan*) in the 1972–73 Estimates.

Displacement	4 000 tons surface, 4 500 tons submerged
Dimensions	$272 \times 33\frac{1}{3} \times 28$ feet
Tubes	Five 21-inch homing
Machinery	1 pressurized water-cooled nuclear reactor
	Geared steam turbines, 1 shaft, speed = up to 35 knots submerged
Complement	97

Name	No.	Builders	Ordered	Laid down	Launched
Sceptre	S 110	Vickers Ltd SB Group, Barrow	7 Sep. 1971		
Sovereign	S 108	Vickers Ltd SB Group, Barrow	16 May 1969	18 Sep. 1970	17 Feb.1973
Superb	S 109	Vickers Ltd SB Group, Barrow	20 May 1970	16 Mar. 1973	
Swiftsure	S 126	Vickers Ltd SB Group, Barrow	3 Nov. 1967	6 June 1969	7 Sep. 1971

Spartan was ordered on 17 February 1973 (announced). Commissioning date for *Swiftsure* was 17 April 1973.

SWIFTSURE *Official*

CHURCHILL   CONQUEROR   COURAGEOUS   VALIANT   WARSPITE

HMS *Valiant* is the first nuclear powered submarine of all-British construction, including the propulsion plant. Her hull is broadly of the same design as that of *Dreadnought,* the prototype nuclear powered submarine built for the Royal Navy, but she is slightly larger. She is armed with homing torpedoes and is equipped to hunt and kill enemy submarines and surface warships, with sonar gear to detect at much greater ranges than that fitted in British conventional submarines.

Displacement	3 500 tons standard, 4 000 tons surface, 4 500 tons submerged
Dimensions	285 $\times 33\frac{1}{4} \times 27$ feet
Tubes	Six 21-inch
Machinery	British prototype pressurized water-cooled nuclear reactor
	Geared steam turbines, 1 shaft, speed $=$ 30 knots
Complement	103

	No.	Builders	Laid Down	Launched	Completed
Churchill	S 46	Vickers-Armstrongs, Ltd, Barrow-in-Furness	30 June 1967	20 Dec. 1968	15 July 1970
Conqueror	S 105	Cammell, Laird & Co. Ltd, Birkenhead	5 Dec. 1967	28 Aug. 1969	9 Nov. 1971
Courageous	S 50	Vickers-Armstrongs, Ltd, Barrow-in-Furness	15 May 1968	7 Mar.1970	16 Oct. 1971
Valiant	S 102	Vickers-Armstrongs, Ltd, Barrow-in-Furness	22 Jan. 1962	3 Dec. 1963	18 July 1966
Warspite	S 103	Vickers-Armstrongs, Ltd, Barrow-in-Furness	10 Dec. 1963	25 Sep. 1965	18 Apr. 1967

The name originally chosen for the second nuclear powered fleet submarine, *Valiant,* was *Inflexible.* The name chosen for the sixth nuclear powered fleet submarine, *Courageous,* was *Superb* (later given to the ninth nuclear powered fleet submarine). On 25 April 1967 *Valiant* completed the 12 000 miles homeward voyage from Singapore after 28 days non-stop, the then record submerged passage by a British submarine.

CHURCHILL

Official

DREADNOUGHT

The Royal Navy's first nuclear powered submarine, specially designed to hunt and destroy enemy underwater craft. A prominent feature of her design is her whale-shaped hull, the near-perfect streamlining giving maximum underwater efficiency, while the fin-like conning tower is also aimed at reducing 'drag' to a minimum. She is capable of continuous high underwater speed combined with long endurance. Her hull is British-built but the nuclear plant was manufactured in the United States, enabling the prototype nuclear powered submarine to be launched much sooner than would otherwise have been the case and giving the Royal Navy earlier operational experience.

Pennant no.	S 101
Displacement	3 000 tons standard, 3 500 tons surface, 4 000 tons submerged
Dimensions	$265\frac{3}{4} \times 32\frac{1}{4} \times 26$ feet
Tubes	Six 21-inch
Machinery	Pressurized water nuclear reactor
	Geared steam turbines, 1 shaft, speed = 30 knots approx.
Complement	88
Builders	Vickers-Armstrongs, Ltd, Barrow-in-Furness
Laid down	12 June 1959
Launched	21 Oct. 1960
Completed	17 Apr. 1963

Most of the names selected for British nuclear powered submarines are former battleship names. The exceptions are *Courageous,* former aircraft carrier (ex-cruiser) name, *Sceptre,* former submarine (and destroyer) name, and *Churchill,* named in honour of the late Sir Winston Churchill, First Lord of the Admiralty during the early part of both the First World War and the Second World War, famous wartime leader and greatest Prime Minister.

DREADNOUGHT *Official*

OBERON ODIN ONSLAUGHT OPOSSUM ORACLE OSIRIS
OCELOT OLYMPUS ONYX OPPORTUNE ORPHEUS OTTER
OTUS

This 'Oberon' class, now officially known as patrol submarines, have improved detection equipment and are capable of high underwater speeds. They are able to maintain continuous submerged patrols in any part of the world and are equipped to fire homing torpedoes. For the first time in British submarines plastic was used in the superstructure construction.

Displacement	1 610 tons standard, 2 030 tons surface, 2 410 tons submerged
Dimensions	$295\frac{1}{4} \times 26\frac{1}{2} \times 18$ feet
Tubes	Eight 21-inch
Machinery	Admiralty Standard Range diesels, 2 shafts, bhp: 3 680 = 12 knots surface
	Electric drive, shp: 6 000 = 17 knots submerged
Complement	68

	No.	Builders	Laid down	Launched	Completed
Oberon	S 09	HM Dockyard, Chatham	28 Nov. 1957	18 July 1959	24 Feb. 1961
Ocelot	S 17	HM Dockyard, Chatham	17 Nov. 1960	5 May 1962	31 Jan. 1964
Odin	S 10	Cammell, Laird & Co. Ltd, Birkenhead	27 Apr. 1959	4 Nov. 1960	3 May 1962
Olympus	S 12	Vickers-Armstrongs, Ltd, Barrow-in-Furness	4 Mar. 1960	14 June 1961	7 July 1962
Onslaught	S 14	HM Dockyard, Chatham	8 Apr. 1959	24 Sep. 1960	14 Aug. 1962
Onyx	S 21	Cammell, Laird & Co. Ltd, Birkenhead	16 Nov. 1964	16 Aug. 1966	20 Nov. 1967
Opossum	S 19	Cammell, Laird & Co. Ltd, Birkenhead	21 Dec. 1961	23 May 1963	5 June 1964
Opportune	S 20	Scotts' Shipbuilding & Engineering Co. Ltd, Greenock	26 Oct. 1962	14 Feb. 1964	29 Dec. 1964
Oracle	S 16	Cammell, Laird & Co., Birkenhead	26 Apr. 1960	26 Sep. 1961	14 Feb. 1963
Orpheus	S 11	Vickers-Armstrongs, Ltd, Barrow-in-Furness	16 Apr. 1959	17 Nov. 1959	25 Nov. 1960
Osiris	S 13	Vickers-Armstrongs, Ltd, Barrow-in-Furness	26 Jan. 1962	29 Nov. 1962	11 Jan. 1964
Otter	S 15	Scotts' Shipbuilding & Engineering Co. Ltd, Greenock	14 Jan. 1960	15 May 1961	20 Aug. 1962
Otus	S 18	Scotts' Shipbuilding & Engineering Co. Ltd, Greenock	31 May 1961	17 Oct. 1962	5 Oct. 1963

OBERON

CACHALOT FINWHALE   GRAMPUS NARWHAL   PORPOISE RORQUAL   SEALION WALRUS

Porpoise was the first operational submarine designed since the Second World War to be accepted into service. The design of hull and superstructure gives high underwater speed and great diving depth. Long endurance, surface and submerged, whether on batteries or snorting. Air and surface warning radar operate at periscope depth as well as when surfaced. Habitability is of highest standard with air conditioning for Arctic or tropical service : oxygen replenishment and carbon dioxide and hydrogen eliminators make it possible to remain totally submerged without even using snort for several days. Apparatus to distil fresh water from sea water and stowage for large quantities of stores and provisions enable this 'Porpoise' class to remain on patrol for months without outside support.

Displacement	1 605 tons standard, 2 030 tons surface, 2 405 tons submerged
Dimensions	$295\frac{1}{4} \times 26\frac{1}{2} \times 18$ feet
Tubes	Eight 21-inch
Machinery	2 ASR 1 turbocharged 16 cyl. diesel generator sets,
	2 shafts, bhp : 3 680 = 12 knots surface
	2 main batteries. Electric drive. hp : 6 000 = 17 knots submerged
Complement	71

	No.	Builders	Laid down	Launched	Completed
Cachalot	S 06	Scotts' Shipbuilding & Engineering Co. Ltd, Greenock	1 Aug. 1955	11 Dec. 1957	1 Sep. 1959
Finwhale	S 05	Cammell, Laird & Co. Ltd, Birkenhead	18 Sep. 1956	30 May 1957	19 Aug. 1960
Grampus	S 04	Cammell, Laird & Co. Ltd, Birkenhead	16 Apr. 1955	21 July 1959	19 Dec. 1958
Narwhal	S 03	Vickers-Armstrongs, Ltd, Barrow-in-Furness	15 Mar. 1956	25 Oct. 1957	4 May 1959
Porpoise	S 01	Vickers-Armstrongs, Ltd, Barrow-in-Furness	15 June 1954	25 Apr. 1956	17 Apr. 1958
Rorqual	S 02	Vickers-Armstrongs, Ltd, Barrow-in-Furness	15 Jan. 1955	5 Dec. 1956	24 Oct. 1958
Sealion	S 07	Cammell, Laird & Co. Ltd, Birkenhead	5 June 1958	31 Dec. 1959	25 July 1961
Walrus	S 08	Scotts' Shipbuilding & Engineering Co. Ltd, Greenock	12 Feb. 1958	22 Sep. 1959	10 Feb. 1961

SEALION *Official*

AENEAS ALCIDE ALLIANCE ANDREW ARTEMIS AURIGA

These 'A' class submarines were originally designed for service in the Pacific, and had a hull different from that of the 'T' class. Construction was entirely welded. All are fitted with 'Snort' breathing equipment. *Alliance* and *Ambush* so fitted remained submerged for record periods in 1947–48. On 15 June 1953 *Andrew* completed a 2 500 sea miles underwater voyage from Bermuda to the English Channel in 15 days, a record for 'snorting' in the Royal Navy. All converted (modernized) since 1955. *Aurochs,* the only unit of the class not rebuilt and streamlined, was scrapped in 1966. *Alderney* was officially listed for disposal in 1968, *Artful* in 1969, *Alcide* in 1970, *Acheron* in 1971 and *Artemis* in 1972, but *Acheron, Alcide, Artemis, Artful* and *Astute* were still in the most recently published Navy List at the time of writing, when officially *Andrew* is operational, *Alliance* is instructional, *Auriga* is in reserve and *Aeneas* is for disposal. *Anchorite* and *Astute* were scrapped in 1970 and *Alaric, Ambush* and *Amphion* in 1971, but building dates for the most recently discarded are included in the table below for the record.

Displacement	1 120 tons standard, 1 385 tons surface, 1 620 tons submerged
Dimensions	$283 \times 22\frac{1}{4} \times 17$ feet
Tubes	Six 21-inch
Machinery	8 cyl. diesel, bhp : 4 300 = 19 knots surface
	Electric motors, hp : 1 250 = 8 knots submerged
Complement	60 to 68

	No.	Builders	Laid down	Launched	Completed
Acheron	S 61	HM Dockyard, Chatham	26 Aug. 1944	25 Mar. 1947	17 Apr. 1948
Aeneas	S 72	Cammell, Laird & Co. Ltd, Birkenhead	10 Oct. 1944	25 Oct. 1945	31 July 1946
Alaric	S 41	Cammell, Laird & Co. Ltd, Birkenhead	31 May 1944	18 Feb. 1946	11 Dec. 1946
Alcide	S 65	Vickers-Armstrongs Ltd, Barrow-in-Furness	2 Jan. 1945	12 Apr. 1945	18 Oct. 1946
Alliance	S 67	Vickers-Armstrongs Ltd, Barrow-in-Furness	13 Mar. 1945	28 July 1945	14 May 1947
Ambush	S 68	Vickers-Armstrongs Ltd, Barrow-in-Furness	17 May 1945	24 Sep. 1945	22 July 1947
Amphion	S 43	Vickers-Armstrongs Ltd, Barrow-in-Furness	14 Nov. 1943	31 Aug. 1944	27 Mar. 1945
Andrew	S 63	Vickers-Armstrongs Ltd, Barrow-in-Furness	13 Aug. 1945	6 Apr. 1946	16 Mar. 1948
Artemis	S 49	Scotts' Shipbuilding & Engineering Co. Ltd, Greenock	28 Feb. 1944	26 Aug. 1946	15 Aug. 1947
Artful	S 96	Scotts' Shipbuilding & Engineering Co. Ltd, Greenock	8 June 1944	22 May 1947	23 Feb. 1948
Astute	S 47	Vickers-Armstrongs Ltd, Barrow-in-Furness	4 Apr. 1944	30 Jan. 1945	30 June 1945
Auriga	S 69	Vickers-Armstrongs Ltd, Barrow-in-Furness	7 June 1944	29 Mar. 1945	12 Jan. 1946

ANDREW

TABARD   TIPTOE

Officially described as 'patrol' submarines for general service. Of saddle-tank design, they originally had an endurance equal to a 42-day patrol. All were subsequently equipped with 'snort'. Of the thirteen residual boats of this class five were modernized and streamlined and eight were fully converted and rebuilt into the most advanced operational submarines, and from them were developed the 'Porpoise' and 'Oberon' classes. The 'streamlines' *Tapir, Teredo* and *Tireless* were removed from the Navy List in 1968, and of the 'conversions' *Totem, Truncheon* and *Turpin* were transferred to the Israeli Navy in 1965–68. *Talent, Thermopolae* and *Token* were listed for disposal in 1968, *Tabard* in 1969, *Tiptoe* in 1970 and *Taciturn* and *Trump* in 1971, but *Taciturn, Talent, Thermopolae, Tiptoe, Token* and *Trump* were still in the 1972 Navy List and *Tabard* was still Submarine Command's show and demonstration boat at HMS *Dolphin,* Fort Blockhouse, until April 1973, when *Tiptoe* was still in Portsmouth Harbour. Two other submarines of the class are retained in the building table below for the record.

Displacement	*Taciturn:* 1 280 tons standard, 1 505 tons surface, 1 700 tons submerged
	Tabard, Tiptoe, Trump: 1 310 tons standard, 1 535 tons surface, 1 740 tons submerged
Dimensions	*Taciturn:* $287\frac{1}{2} \times 26\frac{1}{2} \times 14\frac{3}{4}$ feet
	Tabard, Tiptoe, Trump: $293\frac{1}{2} \times 26\frac{1}{2} \times 14\frac{3}{4}$ feet
Tubes	Six 21-inch
Machinery	Diesels, bhp: 2 500 = $15\frac{1}{4}$ knots surface
	4 electric motors, hp: 2 900 = 15 to 18 knots submerged
Complement	65

	No.	Builders	Laid down	Launched	Completed
Tabard	S 42	Scotts' Shipbuilding & Engineering Co. Ltd, Greenock	6 Sep. 1944	21 Nov. 1945	25 June 1946
Taciturn	S 34	Vickers-Armstrongs, Ltd, Barrow-in-Furness	9 Mar. 1943	7 June 1944	7 Oct. 1944
Tiptoe	S 32	Vickers-Armstrongs, Ltd, Barrow-in-Furness	10 Nov. 1942	25 Feb. 1944	13 June 1944
Trump	S 33	Vickers-Armstrongs, Ltd, Barrow-in-Furness	31 Dec. 1942	25 Mar. 1944	9 July 1944

TABARD

INVINCIBLE

The intention to have a new type of cruiser was first officially mentioned in 1966, and in 1967 and 1968 it was announced that the design was going ahead. In 1969 it was stated that preparatory work was progressing and in 1970 that the design was being developed by assistance contracts placed with the shipbuilding industry. In 1971 it was stated that work continued on the design of the through-deck cruiser and in 1972 that a further contract with the lead shipbuilders (Vickers) was being placed to cover all the remaining preparatory work. The first firm building information was given in the 1973–74 Supply Estimates, Ministry of Defence, where under HM ships in course of construction or on order 'CAH 01' appeared under 'Cruisers', the hull builders being given as Vickers Ltd Shipbuilding Group, Barrow-in-Furness, and the main machinery manufacturers named as Rolls-Royce (1971) Ltd for gas turbines and David Brown & Co. Ltd for gearing. The artist's impression of the official scheme for this new type of ship issued in 1971 showed that the vessel which had been successively and variously known as command cruiser, helicopter carrier, sea control ship and through-deck cruiser was laid out much the same as a fixed-wing aircraft carrier, with a flat top, an angled deck and all the superstructure, including island control, funnels and masts on the starboard side. This first scheme showed two attenuated pyramidal masts stepped abaft each funnel with the large radar lattice surmountng the after mast, but the official photograph of the model issued in 1973 shows an amended version of the arrangement whereby the very prominent radar has been transferred atop a pedestal spiring from the bridge immediately abaft of which is a new and slender, almost pole, foremast before the forefunnel. So the massive former foremast has become the mainmast and its near twin on the after part of the 'island' has been suppressed, doubtless to give unimpeded after control. The ship will be capable of providing a landing deck and hangar with elevator for helicopters, together with facilities for the command and control of naval and maritime air forces. As the ship is configured for a through-deck, that is a flight deck area and approach unobstructed by superstructure, she could provide a limited run for V/STOL aircraft, and with an angled deck she will be virtually a novel type of light fleet aircraft carrier, but unlike previous ships of the latter type in that she has an open forecastle head. Eventually three ships are envisaged, and completion is expected in 1978 to 1981. They will be the largest warships laid down in Britain for nearly 30 years.

Displacement	19 000 to 22 000 tons unofficially estimated
Dimensions	650 × 84 (hull beam), 100 (flight deck) × 24 feet approximately (all unofficially estimated figures)
Aircraft	Helicopter squadron initially, but capacity estimates vary between eight Harrier aircraft with nine Sea King helicopters and 14 Harriers with six Sea Kings
Guided weapons	1 quadruple Exocet surface-to-surface missile launcher 2 twin Sea Dart surface-to-air missile launchers
Machinery	4 Olympus gas turbines, shp: 112 000 = 30 knots
Ordered	17 April 1973
Laid down	20 July 1973

INVINCIBLE

Official

BLAKE   LION   TIGER

These ships have had a chequered building and conversion history extending over a span of more than 30 years. Begun in the middle, and launched about the termination, of the Second World War, they were suspended in 1946, nominated for resumption in 1954, dismantled in 1955 preparatory to rebuilding to a recast design, and not completed until the turn of the sixties. Even then they served only a few years in their intended roles as 'push-button' cruisers. Early in 1965 *Blake* was taken in hand for conversion into a helicopter carrier and it was completed as such in April 1969, followed by *Tiger* taken in hand in 1968 and completed in 1973; *Lion* was to have been similarly adapted in due course. The limited reconstruction involved the suppression of the after twin 6-inch turret and two twin 3-inch mountings, and the provision of a flight deck and hangar for operating four Sea King helicopters.

Displacement	9 550 tons standard, 12 080 tons full load
Dimensions	566 × 64 × 21¾ feet (length before conversion 555½ feet)
Guns	Two 6-inch, two 3-inch anti-aircraft (after conversion)
Guided weapons	Two quadruple 'Seacat' missile launchers
Aircraft	4 anti-submarine helicopters
Machinery	4 Parsons geared turbines,
	4 shafts, shp: 80 000 = 31.5 knots
Boilers	4 Admiralty 3-drum type
Complement	885

	No.	Builders	Laid down	Launched	Completed
Blake	C 99	Fairfield Shipbuilding & Engineering Co. Ltd, Govan	17 Aug. 1942	20 Dec. 1945	8 Mar. 1961
Lion	C 34	Scotts' Shipbuilding & Engineering Co. Ltd, Greenock	24 June 1942	2 Sep. 1944	20 July 1960
Tiger	C 20	John Brown & Co. Ltd, Clydebank	1 Oct. 1941	25 Oct. 1945	18 Mar. 1959

Rescindment: The conversion of the third ship of this class, HMS *Lion,* into a command helicopter cruiser was cancelled in 1972 when she was declared for disposal, but she was still listed in early 1974. Data where different from above: 9 550 tons standard, 11 700 tons full load displacement; 555½ feet overall length; four 6-inch guns in two twin turrets and six 3-inch guns in three twin mountings; no 'Seacat' missile launchers; 716 officers and ratings.

TIGER *Official*

BELFAST

An improved version of the 'Southampton' class design and the largest cruiser in the Royal Navy. Although designed for 10 000 tons standard displacement she suffered damage during the early part of the Second World War and in the course of repairs her beam was increased and other improvements made which resulted in the tonnage being considerably increased. The span of life of this ship drew to a close when she became flagship of the Commodore Reserve Ships in 1966, and with it an era of British naval history. The particulars below obtained when she was in active commission. Her sister ship *Edinburgh* was lost in action in 1942.

Pennant no.	C 35
Displacement	11 550 tons standard, 14 930 tons full load
Dimensions	$613\frac{1}{2} \times 69 \times 23$ feet
Guns	Twelve 6-inch, eight 4-inch dual-purpose, eight 40-mm anti-aircraft
Machinery	Parsons geared turbines, 4 shafts, shp : 80 000 = 32.5 knots
Boilers	4 Admiralty 3-drum type
Complement	710
Builders	Harland & Wolff, Ltd, Belfast
Laid down	10 Dec. 1936
Launched	17 Mar. 1938
Completed	3 Aug. 1939
Reconstructed	1955–1959

Belfast was the last British conventional cruiser in commission. Of the five other latter survivors of the 60 cruisers in the Royal Navy at the end of the Second World War, *Sheffield* was scrapped in 1967 and *Gambia* in 1968, *Blake* and *Tiger* have been converted into helicopter carrying ships, and their original sister ship *Lion* is for disposal in 1973.
Preservation: HMS *Belfast* was paid off as the accommodation ship for the Reserve Ships Authority at Portsmouth (HMS *Bellerophon*) in March 1971, and on 21 October 1971 she was handed over to the Belfast Trust and became a maritime museum ship on the south bank of the River Thames just above Tower Bridge, when it was officially announced that although no longer a fighting unit she would still be regarded as a ship of the Royal Navy, and she continues to wear the White Ensign.

BELFAST

FEARLESS   INTREPID

The first assault ships for the Royal Navy, and the most versatile ships then designed for amphibious warfare which pioneered a new era in British amphibious capability. They can carry heavy tanks and equipment and land troops of an infantry battalion or Royal Marine commando and their vehicles by landing craft. The latter are carried in the ship's dock and launched from a special compartment in the open stern which can be flooded, enabling the craft to be floated out. Fitted out as Naval Assault Group/Brigade Headquarters Ships.

Displacement	11 060 tons standard, 12 120 tons full load, 16 950 tons ballasted
Dimensions	520 × 80 × 20½ (32 ballasted) feet
Aircraft	5 Wessex helicopters
Landing craft	4 LCM 9s in dock; 4 LCVPs at davits
Guided weapons	4 quadruple 'Seacat' missile launchers
Guns	Two 40-mm anti-aircraft
Machinery	2 steam turbines,
	2 shafts, shp: 22 000 = 21 knots
Vehicles	15 tanks, seven 3-ton and twenty $\frac{1}{4}$-ton trucks
Troops	380 at ship's company standards, 700 overload
Complement	556 (36 officers, 520 ratings). 111 Royal Marines and Army

	No.	Builders	Laid down	Launched	Completed
Fearless	L 10	Harland & Wolff, Ltd, Belfast	25 July 1962	19 Dec. 1963	25 Nov. 1965
Intrepid	L 11	John Brown & Co. Ltd, Clydebank	19 Dec. 1962	25 June 1964	11 Mar. 1967

Flight deck: A valuable feature of these ships is the helicopter platform extending about a third of the length of the ship aft which is also the deckhead of the covered well or dock from which the landing craft are floated out.
Power plant: The main propelling machinery is arranged in two self-contained units, each driving one shaft, the engines and boilers being arranged *en echelon,* the two machinery spaces having one turbine and one boiler in each space, the starboard shaft being longer than the port shaft; this is indicated by the two funnels being staggered across the beam of the ship.
Training role: Since 1972 *Intrepid* has been used for the sea training of young officers under instruction from the Britannia Royal Naval College, Dartmouth, and while she is being refitted *Fearless* will take over, but in most respects the ships are otherwise fully operational.

FEARLESS and INTREPID

Official

BIRMINGHAM CARDIFF COVENTRY GLASGOW NEWCASTLE SHEFFIELD

The first all-gas-turbine-propelled destroyers. The design of this 'Type 42' is a smaller version of that of the original 'Type 82' concept. The gas turbine installation is a development of the prototype system in the small converted experimental frigate *Exmouth*. The benefits of the gas turbine plant include the ability to reach maximum speed rapidly, a reduction in weight and space and a 25 per cent reduction in technical manpower. Provision is made for a high standard of accommodation, with living and working spaces fully air-conditioned. The equipment includes the most up to date sonar systems .The helicopter will carry an air-to-surface weapon for use against lightly defended surface ship targets such as fast patrol boats. The prototype of this new class with the 'Seadart' guided missile as main armament was ordered from Vickers Ltd Shipbuilding Group, Barrow-in-Furness (announced 14 November 1968), for service in 1973. As well as a very effective surface-to-air performance the 'Seadart' has a surface-to-surface capability. All perpetuate the names of cruisers of the First World War (*Cardiff* and *Coventry* ('C' class)) and Second World War (*Birmingham, Glasgow, Newcastle* and *Sheffield* ('Southampton' class)).

Displacement	3 500 tons
Dimensions	410 × 47 × 22 feet
Guns	One 4.5-inch dual purpose, two 20-mm anti-aircraft
Guided weapons	1 twin 'Seadart' missile launcher
A/S weapons	Torpedoes carried by helicopter
Aircraft	1 twin engined anti-submarine helicopter (Lynx)
Machinery	2 gas turbines, shp : 56 000 = 30 knots for full power
	2 gas turbines, shp : 10 000 for cruising
	2 shafts ; controllable pitch propellers
Complement	280 (accommodation for 312)

Name	Builders	Ordered	Laid down	Launched
Birmingham	Cammell, Laird & Co Ltd, SBs, Birkenhead	21 May 1971	Sep. 1971	30 July 1973
Cardiff	Vickers Ltd Shipbuilding Group, Barrow	14 Nov. 1968	Nov. 1971	
Coventry	Cammell, Laird & Co. Ltd, SBs, Birkenhead	21 May 1971	July 1972	
Glasgow	Swan Hunter & Tyne Shipbuilders, Ltd	11 Nov. 1971		
Newcastle	Swan Hunter & Tyne Shipbuilders, Ltd	11 Nov. 1971	Sep. 1972	
Sheffield	Vickers Ltd Shipbuilding Group, Barrow	14 Nov. 1968	15 Jan. 1970	10 June 1971

SHEFFIELD

BRISTOL

The design of this ship was originally intended to be an enlarged version of that of the general purpose frigates of the standard 'Leander' class specifically as a vehicle for the new 'Seadart' guided weapons system, but in the event the design turned out larger than that of the guided missile armed destroyers of the 'County' class, and the type has been referred to as escort cruiser, to which category she more nearly approximates. The ship was designed around a powerful new weapons system, and her hull is capable of sea-keeping and high speeds in all weathers, being fully stabilized to present a steady weapons platform. Known by the Royal Navy as 'Type 82' this ship was first envisaged as the prototype of a production class, and it was officially stated in February 1966 that Type 82 ships were expected to be ordered later that year, but in fact only a single ship of the type was ordered (announced in October 1966). Although accepted from the builders at the end of 1972 the ship was further fitted out with classified equipment in HM Dockyard, Portsmouth, early in 1973. She is now the only ship in the Royal Navy with three funnels, one amidships and two aft abreast just abaft the mainmast.

Pennant no.	D 23
Displacement	5 650 tons standard, 6 750 tons full load
Dimensions	$507 \times 55 \times 22\frac{1}{2}$ feet
Guns	One 4.5-inch dual purpose, two 20-mm
Guided weapons	1 twin 'Seadart' missile launcher aft
A/S weapons	1 single 'Ikara' missile launcher;
	1 'Limbo' three-barrelled depth charge mortar
Aircraft	Facilities for one light helicopter (landing platform for Wasp)
Machinery	2 sets geared steam turbines of 30 000 shp boosted by two gas turbines of 44 600 shp
	2 shafts, shp: 74 600 = 32 knots
Boilers	2
Complement	433
Builders	Associated Shipbuilders (Swan Hunter, Wallsend-on-Tyne)
Laid down	15 November 1967
Named	2 June 1969
Launched	30 June 1969
Completed	15 Dec. 1972 (accepted into HM service from the builders)

BRISTOL *Official*

ANTRIM   FIFE   HAMPSHIRE   LONDON
DEVONSHIRE   GLAMORGAN   KENT   NORFOLK

The largest fleet escorts yet built for the Royal Navy, these ships have the dimensions of ships of the pre-war cruiser category. Although they have conventional 4.5-inch guns they also carry the most up-to-date guided missiles yet supplied to the Fleet. The engines are of most advanced design, 'COSAG' combined steam and gas turbine propulsion, giving them the advantage of being able to develop their full power from cold in a short time and enabling ships lying in harbour without steam to get under way instantly in emergency.

Displacement	5 440 tons standard, 6 200 tons full load
Dimensions	$520\frac{1}{2} \times 54 \times 20$ feet
Guns	Four 4.5-inch dual purpose (only two in 'Exocet' ships)
Guided weapons	1 quadruple 'Exocet' missile launcher (in four latest ships);
	1 twin 'Seaslug' missile launcher; 2 quadruple 'Seacat' missile launchers
Aircraft	Westland Wessex helicopter
Machinery	2 sets geared steam turbines boosted by four gas turbines,
	2 shafts, shp: 60 000 = 32.5 knots
Boilers	2 Babcock & Wilcox
Complement	471

	No.	Builders	Laid down	Launched	Completed
Antrim	D 18	Fairfield Shipbuilding & Engineering Co. Ltd, Govan	20 Jan. 1966	19 Oct. 1967	14 July 1970
Devonshire	D 02	Cammell, Laird & Co. Ltd, Birkenhead	9 Mar. 1959	10 June 1960	15 Nov. 1962
Fife	D 20	Fairfield Shipbuilding & Engineering Co. Ltd, Govan	1 June 1962	9 July 1964	21 June 1966
Glamorgan	D 19	Vickers-Armstrongs Ltd, Newcastle-on-Tyne	13 Sep. 1962	9 July 1964	11 Oct. 1966
Hampshire	D 06	John Brown & Co. Ltd, Clydebank	26 Mar. 1959	16 Mar. 1961	15 Mar. 1963
Kent	D 12	Harland & Wolff, Ltd, Belfast	1 Mar. 1960	27 Sep. 1961	15 Aug. 1963
London	D 16	Swan, Hunter & Wigham Richardson, Ltd, Tyne	26 Feb. 1960	7 Dec. 1961	4 Nov. 1963
Norfolk	D 21	Swan, Hunter & Wigham Richardson, Ltd, Tyne	15 Mar. 1966	16 Nov. 1967	7 Mar. 1970

Surface-to-Surface Missile Conversion: HMS *Norfolk* is the first ship in the Royal Navy to be fitted with surface-to-surface guided missiles. The ship was equipped with a quadruple 'Exocet' launcher in March 1973: it is mounted in the place of the twin 4.5-inch turret in 'B' position, chosen by design as the commanding site immediately before the bridge and super-firing over the gunhouse forward in 'A' position. The 'Exocet' system package is being installed in four ships of this 'County' class, the most recently built four it is expected. With the 'Seaslug' surface-to-air long-range missile launcher aft, the two 'Seacat' short-range missile launchers abaft the after funnel, and the 'Exocet' anti-ship missile launcher forward, the ships will be complete end-to-end guided missile ships.

NORFOLK mounting EXOCET forward

Official

DIAMOND   DUCHESS

These were the largest orthodox destroyers ever built for the Royal Navy and were able to perform a number of roles. Not only did they fill the reconnaissance gap left by the scrapping of cruisers but they could give a good volume of fire power in fleet actions. One of this class was temporarily fitted with a 'Seacat' missile, but this was not pursued, this weapon being reserved for the classes which superseded them. *Duchess* was lent to the Royal Australian Navy in 1964, and purchased in 1972 for conversion into a training ship.

Displacement	2 800 tons standard, 3 600 tons full load
Dimensions	390 × 43 × 18 feet
Guns	Six 4.5-inch, two or six 40-mm anti-aircraft
Tubes	Five 21-inch in *Decoy, Diamond, Diana, Duchess* (removed from the latter in 1970)
A/S weapons	'Squid' triple-barrelled depth charge mortar
Machinery	Parsons double geared reduction geared turbines, 2 shafts, shp : 54 000 = 34.75 knots
Boilers	2 Foster Wheeler in *Dainty, Defender, Diamond, Duchess*
	2 Babcock & Wilcox in *Daring, Decoy, Delight, Diana*
Complement	297

	No.	Builders	Laid down	Launched	Completed
Dainty	D 108	J. Samuel White & Co. Ltd, Cowes, I. of W.	17 Dec. 1945	16 Aug. 1950	26 Feb. 1953
Daring	D 05	Swan, Hunter & Wigham Richardson, Ltd, Tyne	29 Sep. 1945	10 Aug. 1949	8 Mar. 1952
Decoy	D 106	Yarrow & Co. Ltd, Scotstoun	22 Sep. 1946	29 Mar. 1949	28 Apr. 1953
Defender	D 114	Alex. Stephen & Sons, Ltd, Govan	22 Mar. 1949	27 July 1950	5 Dec. 1952
Delight	D 119	Fairfield Shipbuilding & Engineering Co. Ltd, Govan	5 Sep. 1946	21 Dec. 1950	9 Oct. 1953
Diamond	D 35	John Brown & Co. Ltd, Clydebank	15 Mar. 1949	14 June 1950	21 Feb. 1952
Diana	D 126	Yarrow & Co. Ltd, Scotstoun	3 Apr. 1947	8 May 1952	29 Mar. 1954
Duchess	D 154	John I. Thornycroft & Co. Ltd, Woolston	2 July 1948	9 Apr. 1951	23 Oct. 1952

'D' Class Disposals: *Dainty, Daring, Defender* and *Delight* were declared for disposal by scrapping during 1969 to 1970, but all were still in the 1972 Navy List. *Decoy* and *Diana* were sold to Peru in 1969 and refitted by Cammell Laird, Ltd Birkenhead, for delivery to Peru under the new names *Ferre* and *Palacios* respectively; they are retained in the building table above *pour memoire*.

Diamond is harbour training ship at Portsmouth for HMS *Collingwood,* the Weapon and Electrical School at Fareham and HMS *Sultan,* the Royal Naval Marine Engineering School at Gosport, Hants.

DIAMOND

BARROSA   CORUNNA

The four survivors of the later 'Battle' class destroyers, one of the best designs ever built for the Royal Navy, were completely reconstructed in 1961–1962 and converted into fleet radar pickets or aircraft direction destroyers, little remaining of the original ships except hull and propelling machinery, and internally they were entirely rebuilt to give a higher standard of fighting efficiency and accommodation. The operations room was one of the most comprehensive and compact ever contrived in destroyers. Of four sister ships, *Alamein, Dunkirk* and *Jutland* were scrapped in 1965, and *Matapan,* laid up in reserve for several years, has been converted into a sonar trials ship, see page 102.

Displacement	2 780 tons standard, 3 430 tons full load
Dimensions	$379 \times 40\frac{1}{2} \times 17\frac{1}{2}$ feet
Guns	Four 4.5-inch
Guided weapons	1 quadruple launcher for 'Seacat' missiles
A/S weapons	1 'Squid' triple-barrelled depth charge mortar
Machinery	Parsons geared turbines,
	2 shafts, shp : 50 000 = 35.75 knots
Boilers	2 Admiralty 3-drum type
Complement	268

	No.	Builders	Laid down	Launched	Completed
Agincourt	D 86	Hawthorn Leslie & Co., Hebburn-on-Tyne	12 Dec. 1943	29 Jan. 1945	25 June 1947
Aisne	D 22	Vickers Armstrongs Ltd, Newcastle-on-Tyne	26 Aug. 1943	12 May 1945	20 Mar. 1947
Barrosa	D 68	John Brown & Co. Ltd, Clydebank	28 Dec. 1943	17 Jan. 1945	14 Feb. 1947
Corunna	D 97	Swan Hunter & Wigham Richardson Ltd, Tyne	12 Apr. 1944	29 May 1945	6 June 1947

Aisne was for disposal in 1970, but was in the most recently published Navy List ,*Agincourt* is listed as Reserve, and in April 1973 *Barrosa,* accommodation ship for the guided missile destroyer *London* while refitting, and *Corunna,* listed with the guided missile destroyer *Hampshire* while refitting, were still in HM Dockyard, Portsmouth, although both *Barrosa* and *Corunna* had been scheduled for disposal.
'Weapon' Class: Of the last two units of the destroyers earlier converted to radar pickets (of the four—*Battleaxe* was scrapped in 1964 and *Broadsword* was expended as a target in 1968), *Crossbow* has been used as a harbour training ship at Portsmouth since 1967 and *Scorpion* used for Naval Construction Research Establishment trials at Rosyth. Both were still in the most recently published Navy List although previously approved for disposal.

BARROSA *Official*

CAPRICE   CAVALIER

These destroyers of traditional British design and appearance were of emergency war construction. They are the survivors of a group of 32 ships nominally divided into four flotillas each of eight ships, the 'Ca', 'Ch', 'Co' and 'Cr' classes. The latter three flotillas have all been scrapped or transferred to other navies, but the 'Ca' class were modernized and converted into anti-submarine escorts. *Cambrian* and *Carysfort* latterly no longer carried torpedo tubes. *Caesar, Cassandra* and *Cavendish* were disposed of in 1967, when the eighth ship of this class, *Carron,* latterly disarmed and used as a navigation tender, was also discarded.

Displacement	2 106 tons standard, 2 749 tons full load
Dimensions	$362\frac{3}{4} \times 35\frac{2}{3} \times 17$ feet
Guns	Three 4.5-inch, four 40-mm anti-aircraft
Tubes	Four 21-inch
A/S weapons	2 'Squid' triple-barrelled depth charge mortars
Guided weapons	1 quadruple 'Seacat' launcher in *Caprice* and *Cavalier*
Machinery	Parsons geared turbines, 2 shafts, shp : 40 000 = 36.75 knots
Boilers	2 Admiralty 3-drum type
Complement	186

	No.	Builders	Laid down	Launched	Completed
Cambrian	D 85	Scotts' Shipbuilding & Engineering Co. Ltd, Greenock	14 Aug. 1942	10 Dec. 1943	17 July 1944
Caprice	D 01	Yarrow & Co. Ltd, Scotstoun	28 Sep. 1942	16 Sep. 1943	5 Apr. 1944
Carysfort	D 25	J. Samuel White & Co. Ltd, Cowes, I. of W.	12 May 1943	25 July 1944	20 Feb. 1945
Cavalier	D 73	J. Samuel White & Co. Ltd, Cowes, I. of W.	28 Feb. 1943	7 Apr. 1944	22 Nov. 1944

Cambrian and *Carysfort* were for disposal in 1970 and 1971, but both were in the most recently published Navy List at the time of writing : they are retained here for the record of this class representing the last conventional destroyers in the Royal Navy. *Caprice* and *Cavalier* were listed for disposal in the statement on the 1973–74 Defence Estimates. They were the last destroyers at sea that saw active service at the end of the Second World War. In April 1973 *Cavalier* was officially stated to be in reserve at Chatham and *Caprice* was listed under seagoing vessels in harbour.

CAVALIER

Official

PROJECTED 'TYPE 22'

Lead items for a standard frigate officially designated as the 'Type 22' were announced on 26 March 1969. She was projected as the prototype of a new class of fleet frigates intended as successors of the very successful general purpose frigates of the 'Leander' class, the construction of which has ceased with the completion of the scheduled programme of 26 ships. In fact it would appear that the so-called frigates of the 'Type 22' will have propelling machinery similar to that of the considerably larger guided missile armed destroyers of the 'Type 42' or 'Sheffield' class, and most of, if not more than, the fighting power of the 'Type 42'. They will have the same COGOG (combined gas or gas) arrangement of Rolls-Royce marine 'Olympus' gas turbines for full power and Rolls-Royce 'Tyne' gas turbines for cruising at economical speed, and will carry the same 'Lynx' anti-submarine helicopter on a flight deck right aft with adjacent hangar, but there the similarity ends. They will be armed with the 'Sea Wolf' close range ship-to-air guided weapon system for launching anti-aircraft missiles (instead of the 'Sea Dart' medium range area defence guided weapon system for launching surface-to-air missiles) disposed in two six-barrelled launchers, one forward (immediately before the bridge in 'B' position) and one aft (*in situ* with the hangar in 'X' position and superfiring over the helicopter flight deck) ; most important, they will carry the package guided weapon system of 'Exocet' surface-to-surface missiles in two twin ramps on the forecastle. They will also mount six short homing torpedo tubes in two triple triangle banks abreast the mainmast. Anti-submarine torpedo tubes will also be dropped from the big helicopter. As can be seen from the artist's impression on the opposite page, the 'Type 22' presents quite an exciting and comprehensive project. In essence this new class of fleet escorts will actually constitute a new category of guided missile ships, and their speed, armament, size, appearance and general utility would seem finally to obviate any distinction between destroyers and frigates as separate categories, the two types having to all intents and purposes merged. It was officially announced in the White Paper Statement on the Defence Estimates 1973-74 issued in February 1973 that 'A contract has been let with Messrs Yarrow for full shipbuilder involvement on the first of a new class of general purpose frigates (the Type 22) with a view to ordering the first ship during the year'.

Displacement	3 000 tons approximately (unofficial estimate)
Aircraft	1 Lynx twin-engined anti-submarine helicopter
Guided weapons	2 twin 'Exocet' surface-to-surface missile launchers
	2 sextuple 'Sea Wolf' surface-to-air missile launchers
Guns	Two 40-mm (single)
Machinery	2-Rolls-Royce Olympus gas turbines, 2 shafts, shp :
	56 000 = 30 knots
	2 Rolls-Royce Tyne gas turbines for economical cruising

TYPE 22

Official

ACTIVE   AMAZON   ANTELOPE   ARROW
ALACRITY   AMBUSCADE   ARDENT   AVENGER

This class of frigates differs from previous classes in several respects, one of the most notable being that the design arose from a private commission instead of a project officially directed to the Royal Corps of Naval Constructors at the Ministry of Defence in Bath. The Navy Department awarded the south coast warship building specialists, Vosper Thornycroft, Ltd, of Portsmouth, Portchester and Southampton, a contract on 27 February 1968 for the design of a patrol frigate to be prepared in full collaboration with Yarrow & Co. Ltd, Glasgow. The resulting first 'Type 21' all-gas-turbine fast frigate, HMS *Amazon*, the name ship of the class, is being completed in 1973. She is the first custom-built gas turbine frigate (designed and constructed as such from the keel up, as opposed to conversion), and the first warship designed by commercial firms and as a collaborative venture for many years. The living accommodation is of a high standard with bunk sleeping, separate dining halls and cafeteria messing. Electric galleys are installed and all quarters, offices and operational spaces are air-conditioned. There is a COGOG (combined gas or gas) arrangement of propelling machinery, with controllable pitch propellers.

Displacement	2 500 tons normal trim
Dimensions	$384 \times 41\frac{3}{4} \times 12\frac{1}{2}$ feet
Aircraft	1 helicopter (equipped initially with Wasp, to be replaced by twin-engined anti-submarine Lynx) launching torpedoes
Guided weapons	1 quadruple 'Seacat' surface-to-air missile launcher (later ships will have 'Seawolf')
Guns	One 4.5-inch, two 20-mm
Machinery	2 Rolls-Royce Olympus gas turbines for full power, 2 shafts, shp : 56 000 = over 30 knots estimated maximum 2 Rolls-Royce Tyne gas turbines for cruising speed
Complement	170

	No.	Builders	Ordered	Laid down	Launched
Active	F 171	Vosper Thornycroft, Ltd, Woolston	30 Apr. 1970	23 July 1971	23 Nov. 1972
Alacrity	F 175	Yarrow & Co. Ltd, Scotstoun	11 Nov. 1971		
Amazon	F 169	Vosper Thornycroft, Ltd, Woolston	26 Mar. 1969	6 Nov. 1969	26 Apr. 1971
Ambuscade	F 172	Yarrow & Co. Ltd, Scotstoun	18 May 1970	June 1971	18 Jan. 1973
Antelope	F 170	Vosper Thornycroft, Ltd, Woolston	30 Apr. 1970	23 Mar. 1971	16 Mar. 1972
Ardent	F 174	Yarrow & Co. Ltd, Scotstoun	11 Nov. 1971	Oct. 1972	
Arrow	F 173	Yarrow & Co. Ltd, Scotstoun	11 Nov. 1971	June 1972	**5 Feb. 1974**
Avenger	F 176	Yarrow & Co. Ltd, Scotstoun	11 Nov. 1971		

(The previous *Amazon* and *Ambuscade* were the rival experimental destroyers built by Thornycroft and Yarrow, respectively, in 1926. *Active, Antelope, Ardent* and *Arrow* revive the names of half of the 'A' class destroyer flotilla completed in 1930. *Alacrity* continues the name of the frigate (sloop) completed in 1945, and *Avenger* of the aircraft carrier completed in 1942 and later the landing ship named in 1947.)

AMAZON

Vosper Thornycroft

ACHILLES APOLLO BACCHANTE DIOMEDE JUPITER
ANDROMEDA ARIADNE CHARYBDIS HERMIONE SCYLLA

These later ships of the numerically large class of general purpose frigates of the 'Leander' type have come to be known as the 'Broad-beam Leanders' as their beam was increased by two feet as compared with the sixteen earlier ships of the group, to improve stability. *Andromeda* was the prototype of the 'broad-beamers'. Actually the ten ships named above constitute the third batch or sub-group of the 'Leander' class with Y 160 machinery as compared with the second series of six ships (*Sirius, Minerva, Phoebe, Danae, Juno, Argonaut*) with Y 136 machinery and the first series of ten ships (*Ajax, Dido, Leander, Penelope, Aurora, Euryalus, Galatea, Arethusa, Naiad* and *Cleopatra*) with Y 100 machinery; but for the 'Ikara' and 'Exocet' conversions vessels may be switched from one batch to another, see pages 60 and 62.

Displacement	2 500 to 2 550 tons standard, 2 962 to 3 000 tons full load
Dimensions	372 × 43 × 18 feet
Aircraft	1 Wasp helicopter armed with homing torpedoes
Guided weapons	1 quadruple 'Seacat' missile launcher
A/S weapons	1 'Limbo' three-barrelled depth charge mortar
Guns	Two 4.5-inch in twin mounting before the bridge, two 20-mm single
Machinery	2 double reduction geared turbines, 2 shafts, shp : 30 000 = 30 knots
Boilers	2 Babcock & Wilcox
Complement	260

	No.	Builders	Laid down	Launched	Completed
Achilles	F 12	Yarrow & Co. Ltd, Scotstoun, Glasgow	1 Dec. 1967	21 Nov. 1968	9 July 1970
Andromeda	F 57	HM Dockyard, Portsmouth	25 May 1966	24 May 1967	2 Dec. 1968
Apollo	F 70	Yarrow & Co. Ltd, Scotstoun, Glasgow	1 May 1969	15 Oct. 1970	17 July 1972
Ariadne	F 72	Yarrow & Co. Ltd, Scotstoun, Glasgow	1 Nov. 1969	10 Sep. 1971	1 Apr. 1973
Bacchante	F 69	Vickers, Ltd, High Walker, Newcastle	27 Oct. 1966	29 Feb. 1968	17 Oct. 1969
Charybdis	F 75	Harland & Wolff, Ltd, Belfast	27 Jan. 1967	28 Feb. 1968	2 June 1969
Diomede	F 16	Yarrow & Co. Ltd, Scotstoun, Glasgow	30 Jan. 1968	15 Apr. 1969	2 Apr. 1971
Hermione	F 58	Alex. Stephen & Sons Ltd, Glasgow	6 Dec. 1965	26 Apr. 1967	11 July 1969
Jupiter	F 60	Yarrow & Co. Ltd, Scotstoun, Glasgow	3 Oct. 1966	4 Sep. 1967	9 Aug. 1969
Scylla	F 71	HM Dockyard, Devonport	17 May 1967	8 Aug. 1968	12 Feb. 1970

APOLLO

ARGONAUT DANAE JUNO PHOEBE
CLEOPATRA DIDO MINERVA SIRIUS

These eight vessels of the early to middle period of the 'Leander' class general purpose frigate building programme have been selected to be converted to surface-to-surface guided missile ships with the installation of the 'Exocet' system contrived by the replacement of the twin 4.5-inch gun mounting before the bridge with a quadruple package launcher. *Cleopatra* will in fact be the first vessel to be equipped with the 'Exocet' long-range anti-ship guided weapons. *Argonaut, Danae, Juno, Minerva, Phoebe* and *Sirius* actually constitute the middle batch of Leanders with Y 136 machinery, and *Cleopatra* and *Dido* belong to the early series with the original Y 100 machinery.

Displacement	2 500 tons standard, 2 900 tons full load
Dimensions	372 × 41 × 18 feet
Guided weapons	1 quadruple 'Exocet' missile launcher (to be installed in lieu of the twin 4.5-inch gun forward)
	1 quadruple 'Seacat' missile launcher
Aircraft	1 helicopter armed with homing torpedoes
A/S weapons	1 'Limbo' three-barrelled depth charge mortar
Guns	Two 20-mm
Machinery	2 double reduction geared turbines, 2 shafts, shp : 30 000 = 30 knots
Boilers	2 Babcock & Wilcox
Complement	260

	No.	Builders	Laid down	Launched	Completed
Argonaut	F 56	Hawthorn Leslie, Ltd, Hebburn-on-Tyne	27 Nov. 1964	8 Feb. 1966	17 Aug. 1967
Cleopatra	F 28	HM Dockyard, Devonport	19 June 1963	25 Mar. 1964	4 Jan. 1966
Danae	F 47	HM Dockyard, Devonport	16 Dec. 1964	31 Oct. 1965	7 Sep. 1967
Dido	F 104	Yarrow & Co. Ltd, Scotstoun, Glasgow	2 Dec. 1959	22 Dec. 1961	10 Dec. 1963
Juno	F 52	John I. Thornycroft, Ltd, Woolston	16 July 1964	24 Nov. 1965	18 July 1967
Minerva	F 45	Vickers Armstrongs, Ltd, Tyne	25 July 1963	19 Dec. 1964	14 May 1966
Phoebe	F 42	Alex. Stephen & Sons Ltd, Glasgow	3 June 1963	8 July 1964	15 Apr. 1966
Sirius	F 40	Dockyard, Portsmouth	9 Aug. 1963	22 Sep. 1964	15 June 1966

ARGONAUT

AJAX AURORA ARETHUSA EURYALUS GALATEA LEANDER NAIAD PENELOPE

As might be deduced from their continued production over several years, the general purpose frigates of the 'Leander' class, which ran into 26 units built from 1959 to 1973, see pages 58 and 60, are one of the most successful classes of warship ever designed. They were developed from the very efficient anti-submarine frigates of the 'Whitby' class, but are of an improved and more versatile type.

Displacement	2 450 tons standard, 2 860 tons full load
Dimensions	372 × 41 × 18 feet
Guns	Two 4.5-inch, two 40-mm anti-aircraft (two 20-mm in 'Seacat' ships)
Guided weapons	1 quadruple 'Seacat' missile launcher
A/S weapons	1 'Limbo' three-barrelled mortar
Aircraft	1 light-weight helicopter armed with homing torpedoes
Machinery	2 sets geared steam turbines, 2 shafts, shp : 30 000 = 30 knots
Complement	263

	No.	Builders	Laid down	Launched	Completed
Leander	F 109	Harland & Wolff, Ltd, Belfast	10 Apr. 1959	28 June 1961	27 Mar. 1963
Ajax	F 114	Cammell, Laird & Co. Ltd, Birkenhead	19 Oct. 1959	16 Aug. 1962	10 Dec. 1963
Penelope	F 127	Vickers-Armstrongs, Ltd, Newcastle-on-Tyne	14 Mar. 1961	17 Aug. 1962	31 Oct. 1963
Aurora	F 10	John Brown & Co. Ltd, Clydebank	1 June 1961	28 Nov. 1962	9 Apr. 1964
Euryalus	F 15	Scotts' Shipbuilding & Engineering Co. Ltd, Greenock	2 Nov. 1961	6 June 1963	16 Sep. 1964
Galatea	F 18	Swan, Hunter & Wigham Richardson, Ltd, Tyne	29 Dec. 1961	28 May 1963	25 Apr. 1964
Arethusa	F 38	J. Samuel White & Co. Ltd, Cowes, Isle of Wight	17 Sep. 1962	5 Nov. 1963	24 Nov. 1965
Naiad	F 39	Yarrow & Co. Ltd, Scotstoun	30 Oct. 1962	4 Nov. 1963	15 Mar. 1965

Conversion: The eight ships of the early 'Leander' class named above, all with Y 100 machinery, were selected for conversion to anti-submarine frigates with the installation of the 'Ikara' long range missile system and launcher capable of delivering homing torpedoes to a position for attacking submarine targets. Propelled by a rocket motor, it will replace the twin 4.5-inch gunhouse immediately before the bridge. *Leander* was thus specially refitted in 1972 and her new armament in addition to 'Ikara' is two 'Seacat' launchers, two multiple 3-inch rocket launchers, 'Limbo' three-barrelled depth charge mortar, two single 40-mm guns and variable depth sonar. She is being followed in the conversion line by *Galatea, Ajax* and *Euryalus,* and the others will be refitted later, including the experimental *Penelope* on completion of 'Seawolf' trials.

LEANDER firing **IKARA**

ASHANTI ESKIMO GURKHA MOHAWK NUBIAN TARTAR ZULU

General purpose vessels designed to fulfil all the functions of frigates rather than to have an outstanding performance in any one specialized role, but capable of carrying out convoy, anti-aircraft and anti-submarine duties. The gas turbines in this 'Tribal' class provide a high concentration of power in a very compact form and are used to supplement the steam turbines for sustained bursts of high speed. They are able to develop full power from cold in a few minutes, providing unprecedented mobility. *Ashanti* and *Gurkha* were fitted with VDS (variable depth sonar) equipment in the counter well in 1970.

Displacement	2 300 tons standard, 2 700 tons full load
Dimensions	$360 \times 42\frac{1}{3} \times 17\frac{1}{2}$ feet
Guns	Two 4.5-inch, two 40-mm anti-aircraft (plus two 20-mm in *Zulu*)
Guided weapons	2 quadruple 'Seacat' launchers in *Ashanti, Gurkha* and *Zulu*
A/S weapons	1 'Limbo' three-barrelled depth charge mortar
Aircraft	1 Westland Wasp helicopter
Machinery	1 Metrovik geared steam turbine, shp: 12 500; 1 Metrovik gas turbine, shp: 7 500
	Total shp: 20 000 = 28 knots
Boilers	1 Babcock & Wilcox, 1 auxiliary
Complement	253

	No.	Builders	Laid down	Launched	Completed
Ashanti	F 117	Yarrow & Co. Ltd, Scotstoun	15 Jan. 1958	9 Mar. 1959	23 Nov. 1961
Eskimo	F 119	J. Samuel White & Co. Ltd, Cowes, I. of W.	22 Oct. 1958	20 Mar. 1960	21 Feb. 1963
Gurkha	F 122	J. I. Thornycroft & Co. Ltd, Woolston	3 Nov. 1958	11 July 1960	13 Feb. 1963
Mohawk	F 125	Vickers-Armstrongs, Ltd, Barrow-in-Furness	23 Dec. 1960	5 Apr. 1962	29 Nov. 1963
Nubian	F 131	HM Dockyard, Portsmouth	7 Sep. 1959	6 Sep. 1960	9 Oct. 1962
Tartar	F 133	HM Dockyard, Devonport	22 Oct. 1959	19 Sep. 1960	26 Feb. 1962
Zulu	F 124	Alex. Stephen & Sons, Ltd, Govan	13 Dec. 1960	3 July 1962	17 Apr. 1964

ZULU

MERMAID

This ship, described in some circles as exotic, controversial and much maligned, was built on quite conventional lines, and is only unusual in that she has had a very chequered construction and delivery history. She was built to the order of the late Dr Kwame Nkrumah, former President of Ghana, as a hermaphrodite state guardship and personal yacht. Specially designed by the Navy Department of the British Ministry of Defence as a combined general purpose frigate/despatch vessel, she was ordered from Yarrow & Co. Ltd, Scotstoun, Glasgow, in 1964. Her main propelling machinery and her hull (but without the 'broken nose' forecastle) were built to conform basically to the standards of the Type 41 British frigates of the 'Leopard' class but with an entirely revised scheme of interior layout and a quite different armament for her primary role for escort, patrol and training and as presidential yacht with generous accommodation for official passengers. The specifications included modern equipment such as the Plessey Radar Naval Package and stabilizers, and the auxiliary machinery comprised four diesel generators. Although broadly similar to the 'Cat' squadron of anti-aircraft frigates in the Royal Navy she had an orthodox funnel and was flush-decked from the helicopter platform at the stern to the shallow sweep up into the bows instead of raised forecastle. She was in an advanced state of construction when President Nkrumah was deposed in 1966 and the contract was rescinded. Nevertheless, to clear the hull off the slip she was proceeded with to the point when she could be launched on Clydeside, and she took the water without ceremony and without name although she was to have been called *The Black Star* (the Ghana flag emblem). In 1968 she was completed for sale abroad but there was no buyer and she was eventually 'bought in, as lying' for the Royal Navy. Towed to Portsmouth in mid April 1972 for survey, she was moved to Chatham later for refit and updating to present British naval standards, having been re-named *Mermaid*, and in the 1973 Defence Estimates listed as a frigate.

Displacement	2 300 tons standard, 2 520 tons full load
Dimensions	340 × 40 × 16 feet
Aircraft	Platform for helicopter
Guns	Two 4-inch in twin mounting
	Two 40-mm single
A/S weapons	One 'Limbo' three-barrelled depth charge mortar
Machinery	8 Admiralty standard range diesels, 2 shafts,
	Controllable pitch propellers, bhp : 14 500 = 25 knots
Complement	210 (original accommodation scheme)
Builders	Yarrow & Co. Ltd, Scotstoun
Launched	29 Dec. 1966
Taken over	October 1972 (for duty in the Royal Navy)
Commissioned	16 May 1973 (after limited modification)
Pennant No	F 76

MERMAID

Wright & Logan

JAGUAR LEOPARD LYNX PUMA

The first rate frigates of this anti-aircraft type, all named after big cats and known as the 'Leopard' class, Type 41, are diesel instead of steam powered. They were designed primarily for the protection of convoys against air attack. They can also serve as a medium type of destroyer in offensive operations. The main armament of two 4.5-inch twin turrets, mountings and gunnery armament control were similar to those mounted in the large destroyers of the 'Daring' class. The secondary armament, initially consisting of two Bofors close-range anti-aircraft pieces, was eventually to be replaced by 'Seacat' ship-to-air guided missile launchers. The ship fabrication was all welded, and the structural arrangements represented the last word in the development of modern technique. *Lynx* and *Puma* were refitted with main 'macks', or combined mast-stacks, in 1963–64 in lieu of the after funnel within lattice, and the other two were similarly restepped, *Leopard* in 1964–66 followed by *Jaguar*. HMS *Puma* was paid off in 1972 and was officially stated to be in reserve at Chatham in 1973, but she was approved for disposal under the 1973–74 Defence Estimates.

Displacement	2 300 tons standard, 2 520 tons full load
Dimensions	340 × 40 × 16 feet
Guns	Four 4.5-inch, one 40-mm anti-aircraft
A/S weapons	'Squid' triple-barrelled depth charge mortar
Machinery	8 Admiralty standard range diesels in three engine rooms, 2 shafts, bhp : 14 400 = 24 knots
Complement	205

	No.	Builders	Laid down	Launched	Completed
Jaguar	F 37	Wm Denny & Bros., Ltd, Dumbarton	2 Nov. 1953	30 July 1957	12 Dec. 1959
Leopard	F 14	HM Dockyard, Portsmouth	25 Mar. 1953	23 May 1955	30 Sep. 1958
Lynx	F 27	John Brown & Co. Ltd, Clydebank	13 Aug. 1953	12 Jan. 1955	14 Mar. 1957
Puma	F 34	Scotts' Shipbuilding & Engineering Co. Ltd, Greenock	16 Nov. 1953	30 June 1954	24 Apr. 1957

JAGUAR

Official

CHICHESTER LINCOLN LLANDAFF SALISBURY

Known as the 'Salisbury' class, these diesel-powered first rate frigates of the aircraft direction category, Type 61, all named after cathedral cities, were designed primarily for the direction of carrier-borne and shore-based aircraft. They could also serve as a lighter type of destroyer in offensive operations. When *Salisbury* underwent extended refit in 1962 her after exhaust or attenuated funnel and main lattice mast combinaton was replaced by a single tall funnel or trunk surmounted by a large air direction aerial reminiscent of the American combined mast and stack or 'mack'. *Chichester* underwent similar reconstruction in 1964 but this was carried further to give her both fore and main 'macks'. *Llandaff* was similarly restepped in 1966, followed by *Lincoln*. The 40-mm gun in *Lincoln* was replaced by a 'Seacat' guided missile quadruple launcher. *Salisbury* was further converted in 1968.

Displacement	2 170 tons standard, 2 350 tons full load
Dimensions	$339\frac{3}{4} \times 40 \times 15\frac{1}{2}$ feet
Guided weapons	1 quadruple 'Seacat' missile launcher in *Lincoln* and *Salisbury*
Guns	Two 4.5-inch in all ships; two 40-mm anti-aircraft (two 20-mm in *Chichester* and *Salisbury*)
A/S weapons	'Squid' triple-barrelled depth charge mortar
Machinery	8 Admiralty standard range diesels in three engine rooms, 2 shafts, bhp: 14 400 = 24 knots
Complement	210

	No.	Builders	Laid down	Launched	Completed
Chichester	F 59	Fairfield Shipbuilding & Engineering Co. Ltd, Govan	25 Jan. 1953	21 Apr. 1955	16 May 1958
Lincoln	F 99	Fairfield Shipbuilding & Engineering Co. Ltd, Govan	20 May 1955	6 Apr. 1959	7 July 1960
Llandaff	F 61	R. & W. Hawthorn Leslie, Ltd, Hebburn-on-Tyne	27 Aug. 1953	30 Nov. 1955	11 Apr. 1958
Salisbury	F 32	HM Dockyard, Devonport	23 Jan. 1952	25 June 1953	27 Feb. 1957

Guardship Modification: During refit in 1972 at Rosyth all the aircraft direction-finding gear in HMS *Chichester*, including the massive radar antennae, was removed, and the 'Seacat' missile launcher was replaced by Bofors and Oerlikon guns. She left Portsmouth in January 1973 for duties as the guardship at Hong Kong in the spring. She is expected to stay in the Far East several years and may never return to Britain. Changes were made for the comfort of the ship's company in the particular climate, with full air-conditioning and additional recreational spaces.

CHICHESTER

BERWICK FALMOUTH LOWESTOFT RHYL YARMOUTH
BRIGHTON LONDONDERRY PLYMOUTH ROTHESAY

These first rate anti-submarine frigates of the advanced 'quality' type (Modified Type 12) officially known as the 'Rothesay' class were basically similar to the 'Whitby' class in design but incorporated modifications in layout as a result of experience gained with the earlier ships of the original Type 12. There were several differences including the single Bofors gun, fitted temporarily to be replaced by the 'Seacat' guided weapon, and the build-up of the after superstructure around the mainmast. In 1966–72 all the ships of this class were reconstructed with hangar and helicopter pad aft, as well as 'Seacat' and variable depth sonar.

Displacement	2 380 tons standard, 2 800 tons full load
Dimensions	370 × 41 × 17⅓ feet
Aircraft	1 Wasp helicopter armed with homing torpedoes
Guns	Two 4.5-inch (twin), two 20-mm single
Guided weapons	1 quadruple 'Seacat' launcher
A/S weapons	1 'Limbo' three-barrelled depth charge mortar
Machinery	2 sets double reduction geared steam turbines, 2 shafts, shp : 30 000 = 30 knots
Boilers	2 Babcock & Wilcox
Complement	235

	No.	Builders	Laid down	Launched	Completed
Berwick	F 115	Harland & Wolff, Ltd, Belfast	16 June 1958	15 Dec. 1958	1 June 1961
Brighton	F 106	Yarrow & Co. Ltd, Scotstoun	23 July 1957	30 Oct. 1959	28 Sep. 1961
Falmouth	F 113	Swan, Hunter & Wigham Richardson, Ltd, Tyne	23 Nov. 1957	15 Dec. 1959	25 July 1961
Londonderry	F 108	J. Samuel White & Co. Ltd, Cowes, I. of W.	15 Nov. 1956	20 May 1958	22 July 1960
Lowestoft	F 103	Alex. Stephen & Sons, Ltd, Govan	9 June 1958	23 June 1960	18 Oct. 1961
Plymouth	F 126	HM Dockyard, Devonport	1 July 1958	20 July 1959	11 May 1961
Rothesay	F 107	Yarrow & Co. Ltd, Scotstoun	6 Nov. 1956	9 Dec. 1957	23 Apr. 1960
Rhyl	F 129	HM Dockyard, Portsmouth	29 Jan. 1958	23 Apr. 1959	31 Oct. 1960
Yarmouth	F 101	John Brown & Co. Ltd, Clydebank	29 Nov. 1957	23 Mar. 1959	26 Mar. 1960

BRIGHTON *Official*

BLACKPOOL   SCARBOROUGH   TORQUAY
EASTBOURNE   TENBY   WHITBY

Primarily designed for the location and destruction of the most modern submarines, these first rate frigates of anti-submarine 'quality' type (Type 12) constituting the 'Whitby' class were fitted with the latest underwater detection equipment and anti-submarine weapons of post-war development. Good sea-keeping qualities enable the vessels to maintain their high speed in rough seas. *Blackpool* was hired to New Zealand for four to five years until a new frigate was built for the Royal New Zealand Navy. She was commissioned as a unit of the Royal New Zealand Navy on 16 June 1966, but returned to the Royal Navy in April 1971 : her disposal was under review but she was still in the most recently published Navy List. *Eastbourne, Scarborough, Tenby* and *Torquay* constituted the Dartmouth Training Squadron, but *Tenby* was paid off early in 1973 and she and *Scarborough* were officially approved for disposal in the 1973–74 Defence Estimates. *Eastbourne* and *Torquay* are engaged on trials and training. In 1972 *Torquay* was refitted and installed with the first complete CAAIS (Computer Assisted Action Information System) to go to sea. *Whitby* was guardship at Hong Kong from end of 1972 to early 1973 until relieved by *Chichester*, see page 70.

Displacement	2 150 tons standard, 2 560 tons full load
Dimensions	$369\frac{3}{4} \times 41 \times 17\frac{1}{2}$ feet
Guns	Two 4.5-inch, two 40-mm anti-aircraft (one 40-mm in Dartmouth Squadron)
A/S weapons	2 'Limbo' three-barrelled depth charge mortars
Machinery	2 sets double reduction geared steam turbines, 2 shafts, shp : 30 430 = 31 knots
Boilers	2 Babcock & Wilcox
Complement	221

	No.	Builders	Laid down	Launched	Completed
Blackpool	F 77	Harland & Wolff, Ltd, Belfast	20 Dec. 1954	14 Feb. 1957	13 Aug. 1958
Eastbourne	F 73	Vickers-Armstrongs, Ltd, Newcastle-on-Tyne	13 Jan. 1954	29 Dec. 1955	9 Jan. 1958
Scarborough	F 63	Vickers-Armstrongs, Ltd, Newcastle-on-Tyne	11 Sep. 1953	4 Apr. 1955	10 May 1957
Tenby	F 65	Cammell, Laird & Co. Ltd, Birkenhead	23 June 1953	4 Oct. 1955	18 Dec. 1957
Torquay	F 43	Harland & Wolff, Ltd, Belfast	11 Mar. 1953	1 July 1954	10 May 1956
Whitby	F 36	Cammell, Laird & Co. Ltd, Birkenhead	30 Sep. 1952	2 July 1954	19 July 1956

TORQUAY

BLACKWOOD DUNDAS HARDY KEPPEL PALLISER
DUNCAN EXMOUTH MALCOLM RUSSELL

All named after captains famous in British naval history, these second rate anti-submarine frigates of 'utility' design (Type 14), constituting the 'Blackwood' class, are very lightly armed, as far as guns are concerned, being intended for a mainly submarine hunting role. They are of comparatively simple construction. In 1958–59 their hulls were strengthened to stand up to the severe and prolonged sea and weather conditions on fishery protection duties in Icelandic waters. In 1966–68 *Exmouth* was converted to all-gas-turbine propulsion. *Murray* and *Pellew* were scrapped in 1971. *Grafton* and *Blackwood* were approved for disposal under the 1970–71 Defence Estimates, but *Grafton* was still in the most recently published Navy List, and *Blackwood* became harbour training ship at Portsmouth for the shore establishments *Sultan* and *Collingwood. Duncan* was harbour training ship for HMS *Caledonia*, the Royal Naval Engineering School at Rosyth, and reserve in 1972. *Malcolm* was scheduled for disposal under the 1973–74 Estimates. All names are retained in the building table to show the class intact.

Displacement	1 180 tons standard, 1 456 tons full load
Dimensions	310 × 33 × 15½ feet
Guns	Two 40-mm anti-aircraft
A/S weapons	2 'Limbo' three-barrelled depth charge mortars
Machinery	1 set geared steam turbines,
	1 shaft, shp : 15 000 = 27.8 knots (*Exmouth* gas turbines)
Boilers	2 Babcock & Wilcox
Complement	140

	No.	Builders	Laid down	Launched	Completed
Blackwood	F 78	John I. Thornycroft & Co. Ltd, Southampton	14 Sep. 1953	4 Oct. 1955	22 Aug. 1957
Duncan	F 80	John I. Thornycroft & Co. Ltd, Southampton	17 Dec. 1953	30 May 1957	21 Oct. 1958
Dundas	F 48	J. Samuel White & Co. Ltd, Cowes, Isle of Wight	17 Oct. 1952	25 Sep. 1953	16 Mar. 1956
Exmouth	F 84	J. Samuel White & Co. Ltd, Cowes, Isle of Wight	24 Mar. 1954	16 Nov. 1955	20 Dec. 1957
Grafton	F 51	J. Samuel White & Co. Ltd, Cowes, Isle of Wight	25 Feb. 1953	13 Sep. 1954	8 Jan. 1957
Hardy	F 54	Yarrow & Co. Ltd, Scotstoun, Glasgow	4 Feb. 1953	25 Nov. 1953	15 Dec. 1955
Keppel	F 85	Yarrow & Co. Ltd, Scotstoun, Glasgow	27 Mar. 1953	31 Aug. 1954	6 July 1956
Malcolm	F 88	Yarrow & Co. Ltd, Scotstoun, Glasgow	1 Feb. 1954	18 Oct. 1955	12 Dec. 1957
Murray	F 91	Alex. Stephen & Sons, Ltd, Govan, Glasgow	30 Nov. 1953	22 Feb. 1955	5 June 1956
Palliser	F 94	Alex. Stephen & Sons, Ltd, Govan, Glasgow	15 Mar. 1955	10 May 1956	13 Dec. 1957
Pellew	F 62	Swan, Hunter & Wigham Richardson, Ltd, Tyne	5 Nov. 1953	29 Sep. 1954	26 July 1956
Russell	F 97	Swan, Hunter & Wigham Richardson, Ltd, Tyne	11 Nov. 1953	10 Dec. 1954	7 Feb. 1957

EXMOUTH *Official*

GRENVILLE   RAPID   ULSTER   UNDAUNTED

Known as the 'full conversion' class and officially listed as 'Type 15', these vessels represented the British post-war conception of fast anti-submarine frigates, and were in the nature of a stop-gap until sufficient anti-submarine frigates could be built. Originally completed during the Second World War as destroyers of the 'T', 'U', 'V', 'W', and 'Z' flotillas, they underwent a complete reconstruction involving stripping down to deck level, extending the forecastle deck right aft, erecting new super-structure and mounting an entirely new armament. Altogether 33 destroyers were converted into fast anti-submarine frigates but only the three above remain of the 'Type 15', only *Rapid* of the four 'Early Type 15' remains, while *Terpsichore* was the last survivor of the seven 'Type 16' of 'limited conversion', the remainder having been scrapped or transferred to other countries. Several of the 'Type 15' were scheduled for disposal in 1969–71 but were still in the most recently published Navy List at the time of writing and are retained in the building table for the record. *Volage* was used as a harbour training ship at Portsmouth for Royal Marines and Sea Cadet forces in Hampshire until relieved in 1973 by *Ulster* (eventually for disposal). *Grenville* is now classified as a Trials Ship.

Displacement	2 240 tons standard, 2 880 tons full load (ships vary)
Dimensions	$362\frac{3}{4}$ (R class $358\frac{1}{4}$) × 35 × 17 feet
Guns	Two 4-inch, two 40-mm anti-aircraft (ships vary)
A/S weapons	'U' class, *Troubridge* and *Zest* : 2 'Limbo' three-barrelled mortars
	'V' and 'W' class : 2 'Squid' triple-barrelled mortars
Tubes	Provisions for tubes. 8 homing torpedo tubes in *Ulster*
Machinery	Parsons geared turbines,
	2 shafts, shp : 40 000 = 36.75 knots designed, 31.25 knots sea speed
Boilers	2 Admiralty 3-drum type
Complement	195

	No.	Builders	Laid down	Launched	Completed
Grenville	F 197	Swan, Hunter & Wigham Richardson, Ltd, Tyne	1 Nov. 1941	12 Oct. 1942	27 May 1943
Troubridge	F 09	John Brown & Co. Ltd, Clydebank	10 Nov. 1941	23 Sep. 1942	8 Mar. 1943
Ulster	F 83	Swan, Hunter & Wigham Richardson, Ltd, Tyne	12 Nov. 1941	9 Nov. 1942	30 June 1943
Undaunted	F 53	Cammell, Laird & Co. Ltd, Birkenhead	8 Sep. 1942	19 July 1943	3 Mar. 1944
Verulam	F 29	Fairfield Shipbuilding & Engineering Co. Ltd, Govan	26 Jan. 1942	22 Apr. 1943	10 Dec. 1943
Wakeful	F 159	Fairfield Shipbuilding & Engineering Co. Ltd, Govan	3 June 1942	30 Jan. 1943	17 Feb. 1944
Whirlwind	F 187	R. & W. Hawthorn, Leslie & Co. Ltd, Tyne	31 July 1942	30 Aug. 1943	20 July 1944
Zest	F 102	John I. Thornycroft & Co. Ltd, Woolston	21 July 1942	14 Oct. 1943	20 July 1944
Rapid	F 138	Cammell, Laird & Co. Ltd, Birkenhead	16 June 1941	16 July 1942	20 Feb. 1943
Relentless	F 185	John Brown & Co. Ltd, Clydebank	20 June 1941	15 July 1942	30 Nov. 1942

GRENVILLE   *Official*

SIR BEDIVERE
SIR GALAHAD

SIR GERAINT
SIR LANCELOT

SIR PERCIVAL
SIR TRISTRAM

Sir Lancelot was the prototype of a new class of ship to replace tank landing ships of the LST(3) type for service as a multi-purpose fast troop and roll-on/roll-off heavy vehicle carrier. She was built to the order of the Ministry of Transport on behalf of the Ministry of Defence (Army) but was transferred to the Royal Fleet Auxiliary Service six years after completion and extensive military probing trials. Fitted for bow and stern loading with drive-through facility and deck-to-deck ramps, the ship is capable of discharging a full load of vehicles on to a beach. Facilities are provided for stowing and operating military pontoon equipment. On-board maintenance of vehicles and equipment and stowage of special military cargo are catered for. A passive tank stabilizer system and bow thrust propulsion unit are fitted. All accommodation is air-conditioned and close circuit television fitted for both operational and recreational use. The five later ships of the production series are similar in size and capacity to the class prototype but with modified layout following experience with *Sir Lancelot,* and the vehicle deck provides increased vehicle stowage and improved night flying facilities forward. Revision of military accommodation and services was carried out, with bridge control of main engines and fitting of machinery and data-logging equipment. These five ships, of which particulars are given below (*Sir Lancelot* differs slightly), have full capability for operating Wessex helicopters (of which 11 can be carried on the tank deck and 9 on the vehicle deck) from both the after landing platform and the foredeck by day or night. All Royal Fleet Auxiliaries since 1970.

Displacement	3 270 tons light, 5 674 tons load
Measurement	4 473 tons gross, 2 404 tons deadweight
Dimensions	412 × 60 × 13 feet mean
Machinery	2 diesels, bhp : 9 400 (8 460 = 17 knots service speed)
Aircraft	Up to 20 Wessex helicopters can be carried
Guns	Two 40-mm
Complement	Crew 68 ; military passengers 340

	No.	Builders	Laid down	Launched	Completed	Listed RFA
Sir Bedivere	L 3004	Hawthorn, Leslie	Oct. 1965	20 July 1966	18 May 1967	14 Jan. 1970
Sir Galahad	L 3005	Alex. Stephen	Feb. 1965	19 Apr. 1966	17 Dec. 1966	7 Mar. 1970
Sir Geraint	L 3037	Alex. Stephen	June 1965	26 Jan. 1967	12 July 1967	5 Mar. 1970
Sir Lancelot	L 3029	Fairfield S & E	Mar. 1962	June 1963	Jan. 1964	3 Jan. 1970
Sir Percival	L 3036	Hawthorn, Leslie	Apr. 1966	4 Oct. 1967	23 Mar. 1968	6 Mar. 1970
Sir Tristram	L 3505	Hawthorn, Leslie	Feb. 1966	12 Dec. 1966	14 Sep. 1967	30 Jan. 1970

(*Sir Lancelot* only : 3 370 light, 5 550 load, 6 390 gross originally, 2 180 deadweight, 2 Denny Sulzer diesels, 9 520 bhp, 8 250 service)

SIR GALAHAD

ABDIEL

This unique ship was designed as an exercise minelayer for the Royal Navy. Her function is to support mine countermeasures forces and to maintain these forces whenever they are operating away from their shore bases, and to lay exercise mines. Her living accommodation is of a high standard. She was built to replace the thirty-year-old coastal minelayer *Plover*, 805 tons standard, 1 020 tons full load, triple expansion steam reciprocating engines, $14\frac{3}{4}$ knots, employed as a tender to HMS *Vernon* shore establishment, the Torpedo and Anti-Submarine School, and to take over the functions of a number of ageing vessels employed on mine control.

Pennant no.	N 21
Displacement	1 375 tons standard, 1 500 tons full load
Dimensions	$265 \times 38\frac{1}{2} \times 10$ feet
Mines	44 carried
Machinery	2 Paxman Ventura 16 cylinder pressure charged diesels, bhp: 2 690 = 16 knots
Complement	123
Builders	John I. Thornycroft & Co. Ltd, Woolston, Southampton
Ordered	11 June 1965
Laid down	23 May 1966
Launched	27 Jan. 1967
Completed	17 Oct. 1967

(The previous ship of the Royal Navy named *Abdiel* was the fast minelayer of 2 650 tons standard displacement, 4 000 tons full load, with a capacity of 108 mines and a speed of 40 knots, completed in April 1941 and sunk by mine in September 1943: of the remainder of this class of six ships, *Latona* and *Welshman* were also lost during the Second World War, *Apollo* and *Ariadne* were scrapped in 1962 and 1963 respectively, and *Manxman*, converted into a minesweeper support ship in 1960–63 but latterly used as a sea training ship for marine engineer officers, was broken up in 1973.)

ABDIEL

ALFRISTON (*Kilmorey*)
ASHTON
BICKINGTON (*Killiecrankie*)
BILDESTON
BOSSINGTON
BRERETON
BRINTON
BRONINGTON
CHAWTON
CRICHTON (*St David*)
CROFTON (*Solent*)
CUXTON

FITTLETON (*Curzon*)
GAVINTON
GLASSERTON
HIGHBURTON
HODGESTON (*Venturer*)
HUBBERSTON
IVESTON
KEDLESTON
KELLINGTON
KIRKLISTON
LALESTON
LEWISTON
MAXTON

NURTON
POLLINGTON (*Mersey*)
REPTON (*Clyde*)
SHERATON
SOBERTON
STUBBINGTON (*Montrose*)
UPTON
WALKERTON
WILTON
WISTON (*Northumbria*)
WOOLASTON (*Thames*)
WOTTON
SHOULTON

These vessels were of a new type with double mahogany hull and constructed of aluminium alloy and other materials with the lowest possible magnetic attraction to attain the greatest possible safety factor when sweeping. John I. Thornycroft & Co. Ltd, Woolston, Southampton, were the 'parent' firm for the group of shipyards which built this numerically large class of uniform design capable of sweeping both contact and influence type mines and dealing with mines operated magnetically and acoustically. The first, *Coniston,* was completed in February 1953; she had Vosper stabilizers and most of the class were subsequently so fitted. A total of 118 units of this class was built of which 35 were transferred to other navies; two were converted into survey ships, *Mermaid* (ex-*Sullington*) and *Myrmidon* (ex-*Edderton*), and 38 were listed for disposal in 1967–73. Eleven units are renamed and attached to Royal Naval Reserve Division Headquarters (see names above). Sixteen have been converted into minehunters. Five were refitted as coastal patrol vessels in 1971, see page 96.

Displacement	360 tons standard, 425 tons full load
Dimensions	$153 \times 28\frac{3}{4} \times 8\frac{1}{4}$ feet
Guns	One 40-mm anti-aircraft (removed in some ships); two 20-mm anti-aircraft (some minehunters have two 40-mm)
Machinery	2 diesels, 2 shafts. Most ships have Deltics, bhp: 3 000, others Mirrlees, bhp: 2 500 = 15 knots
Complement	27 minesweepers, 36 minehunters

Royal Naval Reserve: The names in parentheses above are the names borne while attached to RNR Divisions as follows: London *Thames,* Clyde *Clyde,* Forth *Killiecrankie,* Mersey *Mersey,* Severn *Venturer,* South Wales *St David,* Sussex *Curzon,* Solent *Solent,* Tay *Montrose,* Tyne *Northumbria* and Ulster *Kilmorey.*

WILTON is the world's first glass reinforced plastic warship. She was built to the existing minehunter design by Vosper Thornycroft and her particulars are similar to those of the 'Ton' class. In fact she is fitted with reconditioned machinery and equipment from the scrapped *Derriton.* She was launched on 18 January 1972 and completed by 21 May 1973.

HUBBERSTON

Official

ARLINGHAM	TRV(PAS)	**FORDHAM**	DGV	**PUTTENHAM**	RNXS
BIRDHAM	RNXS	**FRITHAM**	TRV	**SHIPHAM**	RNXS
BUCKLESHAM	TRV	**HAVERSHAM**	TRV	**THAKENHAM**	RNXS
DITTISHAM	TRV	**LASHAM**	TRV	**THATCHAM**	DGV
DOWNHAM	TRV	**ODIHAM**	RNXS	**THORNHAM**	
EVERINGHAM	PAS	**PAGHAM**	RNXS	**TONGHAM**	PAS
FLINTHAM	TRV	**PORTISHAM**	RNXS	**WARMINGHAM**	DGV

These boats were designed to operate in shallow waters, rivers and estuaries. When built they were an entirely new type of naval vessel embodying novel features resulting from lessons learned during the Second World War and in the course of subsequent developments. They were named after villages with the suffix 'ham' and have long been known as the 'Ham' class. The first inshore minesweeper, *Inglesham,* was launched by J. Samuel White & Co. Ltd, Cowes, on 23 April 1952. Some 94 boats were built, of which 36 were transferred to foreign countries, two were loaned to the Royal Air Force, two were converted into inshore survey craft and 33 have been scrapped or otherwise disposed of. The 'M 2601' series were of composite non-magnetic metal and wooden construction whereas the 'M 2701' series were built of wood. Nos. 2777 *et seq.* were very slightly larger overall, see dimensions below. Of the vessels named above most were adapted for the Royal Naval Auxiliary Service (RNXS), employed in the Port Auxiliary Service (PAS), fitted as Torpedo Recovery Vessels (TRV) or converted into Degaussing Vessels (DGV). However, *Dittisham* and *Flintham* are in full commission as HM ships and training tenders to HMS *Ganges* shore training establishment, *Thornham* is still in the Navy List as Aberdeen University RN Unit, *Arlingham* is in commission on TRV duties and *Everingham* is also TRV. *Sandringham* is employed on ferry duties, and *Sidlesham* is used as sail training base by the Sussex Constabulary in Chichester Harbour. *Halsham,* former Royal Navy and latterly Royal Air Force, was transferred to the Royal Corps of Transport on 19 December 1972.

Displacement	120 standard, 159 tons full load
Dimensions	$107\frac{1}{2} \times 22 \times 5\frac{3}{4}$ feet
Guns	One 20-mm anti-aircraft (removed in some ships) ; some had one 40-mm anti-aircraft
Machinery	2 Paxman diesels, bhp : 1 100 = 14 knots
Complement	15

AVELEY   **CRADLEY** (*Isis*)

(Of the ten inshore minesweepers of the 'Ley' class (M 2001 series), composite hunters, 123 tons, 164 tons full load, 700 bhp, 13 knots, only two survive, *Aveley* attached to Plymouth, and *Cradley* formerly in London Division RNR and renamed *Isis,* but now Solent Division RNR.)

DITTISHAM

Official

TRIUMPH

The sole representative in the Royal Navy of a highly successful class of light fleet aircraft carriers, although four sister ships are serving in foreign navies. Her reconstruction in HM Dockyard, Portsmouth, spanned nearly seven years, but she was suspended for $2\frac{1}{2}$ years, other commitments having taken priority. Conversion included the complete stripping of the hangar, and workshops were built throughout its entire length. Sponsons were also removed and a large hangar for helicopters was constructed on the flight deck. Following conversion she sailed for the Far East as an escort maintenance ship. She can take four destroyers or frigates alongside, two on each beam.

Pennant no.	A 108 (ex-R 16)
Displacement	13 350 tons standard, 17 000 tons full load after conversion
Dimensions	$699 \times 112\frac{1}{2} \times 23\frac{1}{2}$ feet
Aircraft	3 helicopters in new flight deck hangar
Guns	Four 40-mm anti-aircraft
Machinery	Parsons geared turbines, 2 shafts, shp : 40 000 = 24.25 knots
Boilers	4 Admiralty 3-drum type
Complement	Ship's company 500 plus maintenance staff 285
Builders	R. & W. Hawthorn Leslie & Co. Ltd, Hebburn-on-Tyne
Laid down	27 Jan. 1943
Launched	2 Oct. 1944
Completed	9 Apr. 1946
Converted	1958–1965

HMS *Triumph* returned to Portsmouth on 28 February 1972 from the Far East and arrived at HM Dockyard, Chatham, on **17 March 1972 where she was refitted and still remained in April 1974 as fleet maintenance ship.**
Sister Ships: Of her original sister aircraft carriers, *Glory* was broken up in 1961 and *Ocean* and *Theseus* in 1962. Of her sisters transferred to foreign navies, *Venerable* was sold to the Netherlands in 1948 and renamed *Karel Doorman* and again sold to Argentina in 1968 and renamed 25 *de Mayo, Colossus* was sold to France in 1951 and renamed *Arromanches, Vengeance* was sold to Brazil in 1956 and renamed *Minas Gerais,* and *Warrior* was sold to Argentina in 1958 and renamed *Independencia.*

TRIUMPH

BERRY HEAD   HARTLAND POINT   RAME HEAD

Hartland Point, former landing maintenance ship, was extensively refitted internally and externally and modernized as an escort maintenance ship in 1959–60 for the support of destroyers and frigates in the Far East, but she returned to the United Kingdom in 1965. *Mull of Kintyre,* originally an armament maintenance ship and subsequently a repair and accommodation ship, was converted into a minesweeper maintenance ship in 1961 and based at Singapore. *Berry Head* and *Rame Head,* escort maintenance ships, were refitted and modernized in 1960–63. *Duncansby Head* in 1962 became 'half' of HMS *Cochrane* (Senior Officer Reserve Ships, Rosyth) as a living ship jointly with *Girdle Ness,* former landing craft maintenance ship converted to a guided weapons trials ship in 1953–56 but paid off in 1961 and reclassified as an accommodation ship in 1962.

Displacement	8 580 tons standard, 10 200 tons full load (ships vary)
	Girdle Ness: 10 000 tons standard, 11 620 tons full load (as converted)
Dimensions	$441\frac{1}{2} \times 57\frac{1}{2} \times 22\frac{1}{2}$ feet
Guns	Eleven 40-mm anti-aircraft
Machinery	Triple expansion, ihp: 2 500 = 10 knots
Complement	445 (*Hartland Point* as converted)

	No.	Builders	Laid down	Launched	Completed
Berry Head	A 191	North Vancouver Ship Repairs	15 June 1944	21 Oct. 1944	30 May 1945
Duncansby Head	A 158	Burrard Dry Dock, N. Vancouver	29 July 1944	17 Nov. 1944	8 Aug. 1945
Girdle Ness	A 387	Burrard Dry Dock, N. Vancouver	7 Dec. 1944	29 Mar. 1945	5 Sep. 1945
Hartland Point	A 262	Burrard Dry Dock, N. Vancouver	18 July 1944	4 Nov. 1944	11 July 1945
Mull of Kintyre	A 225	North Vancouver Ship Repairs	21 Dec. 1944	5 Apr. 1945	5 Nov. 1945
Rame Head	A 134	Burrard Dry Dock, N. Vancouver	12 July 1944	22 Nov. 1944	18 Aug. 1945

Duncansby Head, Girdleness and *Mull of Kintyre* were scrapped in 1970, in Spain, Scotland and Hong Kong respectively, but have been retained in the table above for the record.

HARTLAND POINT

Official

DEFIANCE (ex-Forth)   MAIDSTONE

Maidstone was extensively reconstructed in HM Dockyard, Portsmouth, in 1958 to 1962 to act as parent ship for the first British nuclear powered submarine *Dreadnought* and successive nuclear powered submarines, and was modified with lattice foremast and additional superstructure amidships. *Forth* was similarly modernized and converted into a support ship for nuclear powered submarines in HM Dockyard, Chatham, in 1962 to 1966. Both ships, of course, were also capable of supporting conventionally powered submarines. Besides large workshops there were repair facilities on board for all material in the attached submarines and extensive diving and salvage equipment was carried. The original main armament of eight 4.5-inch guns was removed during conversion. *Maidstone* was flagship of the Commander-in-Chief Home Fleet from August 1956 until March 1958. In 1969 she was listed for disposal, but in October that year she was restored and recommissioned as an accommodation ship for 2 000 troops and sent to Belfast where she has remained ever since. In 1972 *Forth* was renamed HMS *Defiance* as the Fleet Maintenance Base at Devonport and parent ship of the 2nd Submarine Squadron.

Displacement	10 000 tons standard, 13 000 tons full load
Dimensions	531 × 73 × 21¼ feet
Guns	Five 40-mm anti-aircraft
Machinery	Geared turbines,
	2 shafts, shp : 7 000 = 16 knots
Boilers	Four Admiralty 3-drum type
Complement	695 ship's company, but accommodation for over 1 500

	No.	Builders	Laid down	Launched	Completed	Rebuilt
Forth	A 187	John Brown & Co. Ltd, Clydebank	30 June 1937	11 Aug. 1938	14 May 1939	1962–1966
Maidstone	A 185	John Brown & Co. Ltd, Clydebank	17 Aug. 1936	21 Oct. 1937	5 May 1938	1958–1962

The larger submarine parent ship *Adamant*, 16 500 tons full load, completed in 1942, was disposed of in late 1970 ; and the large destroyer depot ship *Tyne*, 14 600 tons full load displacement, completed in 1941, was scrapped at Barrow in late 1972.

DEFIANCE (ex-FORTH)

Official

ENDURANCE

This distinctive vessel, formerly the *Anita Dan,* was a ten-year-old ship purchased from J. Lauritzen Lines, Copenhagen. She is specially strengthened for operation in ice. She was converted by Harland & Wolff Ltd, Belfast, into an ice patrol ship for southernmost waters to replace HMS *Protector* and undertake hydrographic and oceanographic surveys for the Royal Navy, acting also as support ship and guard vessel. Her new name *Endurance* was announced on 27 July 1967, and she was ready for deployment in the Antarctic for the 1968 season by October. She is refitted in the United Kingdom each year from May to October during the Antarctic winter. An unusual feature for one of HM ships is the colour of her hull which is painted a vivid red for easy identification in the ice, particularly from the air, but her upperworks and funnel are painted the traditional white and buff of the naval surveying fleet. Another uncommon feature is that the ship can be controlled from the crow's nest in order to give her officers and lookouts the furthest views of channels through the ice.

Pennant no.	A 171
Displacement	3 600 normal tons
Measurement	2 641 tons gross
Dimensions	300 (305 including helicopter deck extension aft) × 46 × 18 (maximum) feet
Aircraft	2 Whirlwind helicopters
Guns	Two 20-mm
Machinery	Burmeister & Wain diesels, 1 shaft, bhp : 3 220 = $14\frac{1}{2}$ knots
Complement	119, including a small Royal Marine detachment, plus 12 spare berths for scientists
Purchased	20 Feb. 1967
Renamed	27 July 1967
Converted	1 Oct. 1968

(The previous ice patrol ship, HMS *Protector,* A 146, built as a netlayer in 1935–36 and converted for service in the Falkland Islands Dependencies in 1955, was paid off in 1968, approved for disposal in 1969 and is laid up. Her original sister ship, the netlayer *Guardian,* was disposed of in 1962.)

ENDURANCE *Official*

BEACHAMPTON   MONKTON   WASPERTON   WOLVERTON   YARNTON

These handy and economical little ships were originally standard coastal minesweepers of the post-war mass production or series type known as the 'Ton' class from their being named after villages with the suffix 'ton', see page 84. At the end of 1971 they were refitted and rearmed as gunboats and were redesignated as coastal patrol vessels, and as a logical consequence they were allocated 'P' Flag Superior pennant numbers instead of 'M' pennant numbers and also renumbered in a new '1 000' series instead of their original '1 100' series, but otherwise retaining the same figures. They were converted and adapted for deployment overseas on patrol and guard duties, a role fulfilled by the class of coastal minesweepers from whence they came ever since the confrontation in the Far East a few years ago.

Displacement	360 tons standard, 425 tons full load
Dimensions	153 × 28¾ × 8¼ feet
Guns	Two 40-mm Bofors, single, one forward and one aft
Machinery	2 diesels. 2 shafts,
	bhp : 3 000 = 15 knots
Complement	30 average

Pennant nos.:			
Beachampton	P 1007 (ex-M 1107)	*Wasperton*	P 1089 (ex-M 1189)
Monkton	P 1055 (ex-M 1155)	*Wolverton*	P 1093 (ex-M 1193)
		Yarnton	P 1096 (ex-M 1196)

CIGNET (P261)   KINGFISHER (P 260)   PETREL (P262)   SANDPIPER (P263)

New construction: Designated the 'Bird' class (similar to the RAF 'Seal' class). Length : 123 feet ; twin screw ; speed : 25 knots. According to the official statement on the 1973 Defence Estimates four new patrol craft would be under construction by 31 March. Hull builders : Richard Dunston (Hessle) Ltd, Hessle. Main machinery manufacturers : Paxman Diesel Ltd, Colchester (main engines) ; Zahnradfabrik, Friedrichshafen, Federal Republic of Germany (gearing).

Seaward Defence Boats: Sole survivors of the 19 boats of the 'Ford' class, *Dee* (ex-*Beckford*) and *Droxford*, are attached to the Mersey and Clyde Divisions of the Royal Naval Reserve and still in the Navy List. Displacement 142 tons full load, dimensions 117¼ × 20 × 7 feet, machinery Davey Paxman diesels (Foden engine on centre shaft), 1 100 bhp = 18 knots, crew 19. Originally designed to locate and destroy submarines, with one 40-mm gun and depth charges.

MONKTON

TENACITY

This handsome and well-found craft was originally designed and built as a private venture by the south coast warship specialists, Vosper Thornycroft Ltd, at their Camber Yard, Portsmouth, to demonstrate the company's latest thinking on the larger type of missile-armed fast patrol boat which has attracted the interest of some 25 navies in recent years. She was intended to be the prototype of a somewhat heavier than usual class of coastal forces craft, constructed with a steel hull, instead of wood, and aluminium superstructure. Her keel was laid very early in 1969 and she was launched in a matter of six weeks or so in mid February and completed only seven months later by the end of the summer to show her paces. As used for demonstration purposes she was fitted with a simulated gun on the forecastle and a mock-up guided missile installation of two twin Seakiller launchers aft. (There were several alternative schemes of armament, according to customers' requirements.) At first the British Ministry of Defence took less interest in her than foreign navies, but she was twice chartered by the Royal Navy, in March 1971 and mid 1971, for NATO exercises with motor torpedo boats, because the Navy had run down its operational coastal forces craft. On 25 January 1972 it was announced that the Ministry of Defence had purchased *Tenacity* outright 'as lying' and since then she has been refitted and modified to meet naval requirements for use on exercises and fishery protection duties. With fully air-conditioned quarters, she is the largest fast patrol boat ever entered for service in the Royal Navy and at the time of writing she is the fastest operational warship at sea.

Pennant no.	P 276
Displacement	165 tons standard, 220 tons full load
Dimensions	$144\frac{1}{2} \times 26\frac{2}{3} \times 7\frac{3}{4}$ feet
Guns	Provision for two light machine guns on bridge sides and small arms, but gun (40-mm or 20-mm) on foredeck is under review
Machinery	3 Rolls-Royce Proteus gas turbines, 3 shafts, bhp: 12 750 = 40 knots for full power; or 2 Paxman Ventura diesels on wing shafts = 16 knots for cruising
Complement	30
Builders	Vosper Thornycroft Ltd, Portsmouth
Launched	18 Feb. 1969
Completed	24 Sep. 1969
Converted	Apr. 1972 to Feb. 1973 by Vosper, Portchester

TENACITY

Vosper

CUTLASS   SABRE   SCIMITAR

These three vessels of recent construction are officially designated as fast training craft and not as fast patrol boats because although built on fast patrol boat or torpedo boat lines they have no armament. With hulls of glued laminated wood construction, their design was developed from that of the 'Brave' class fast patrol boats. They provide anti-fast patrol boat training for the ships and helicopters of the Fleet and for the ships of NATO navies exercising off Portland naval base under the jurisdiction of the Flag Officer Sea Training and in Command Portland Naval Base. They have two sets of propelling machinery installed in a CODOG (combined diesel or gas) arrangement for cruising on the auxiliary drive engines and full power on the main engines. All three were built by Vosper Thornycroft Ltd, at their Portchester Shipyard, having been launched on 4 December 1969 (*Scimitar*), 18 February 1970 (*Cutlass*) and 21 April 1970 (*Sabre*).

Pennant nos.	*Cutlass* P 274, *Sabre* P 275, *Scimitar* P 271
Displacement	102 tons full load
Dimensions	$103\frac{1}{2} \times 27\frac{2}{3} \times 5$ feet
Machinery	2 Rolls-Royce Proteus gas turbines, 2 shafts,
	bhp: 8 500 = 40 knots full power
	2 Foden diesels, bhp: 650 = $11\frac{1}{2}$ knots cruising
Complement	12

There are four fast patrol boats in reserve:
BRAVE BORDERER P 1011 and **BRAVE SWORDSMAN** P 1012, both designed as convertible and interchangeable torpedo boats and gunboats, built by Vosper, Ltd, Portsmouth, and completed in 1960. Displacement 114 tons full load, length 99 feet, beam $25\frac{1}{2}$ feet, draught 7 feet, armament as MTB four 21-inch torpedoes and one 40-mm gun or as MGB two 40-mm guns and two 21-inch torpedoes, machinery 3 Bristol Siddeley Proteus gas turbines, 3 shafts, 10 500 shp = 52 knots, complement 20. Decommissioned in 1970.
DARK GLADIATOR P 1114 and **DARK HERO** P 1115, survivors of a class of 18 convertible gunboats or torpedo boats. Displacement 70 tons full load, length $71\frac{1}{2}$ feet, beam 20 feet, draught 6 feet, armament as MGB one 4.5-inch and one 40-mm gun or as MTB four 21-inch torpedoes and one 40-mm gun, machinery 2 Napier Deltic diesels, 5 000 shp = 46 knots designed, 37 knots sea speed, complement 15. In reserve since 1972. *Dark Adventurer, Dark Hussar* and *Dark Intruder* were also still in the Navy List.

CUTLASS, SCIMITAR and SABRE

MATAPAN

This now completely transformed vessel was originally completed as a standard destroyer of the later 'Battle' class after the Second World War, but she went into reserve almost immediately after her first sea trials, having steamed for a total of only 107 hours. Nearly a quarter of a century later she was taken in hand for reconstruction as a trials ship for underwater weapons. The conversion involved the fitting of a new clipper bow with bulbous forefoot and deep skeg; extending the forecastle deck aft all the way to the counter, thus remodelling her into a flushdecker; erecting a new bridge and forward superstructure; stepping a new plated mast for simpler maintenance and housing compartments associated with signalling; building a second funnel to contain the silencers and exhaust stacks from the diesels driving the extra generators; erecting additional deckhouses on the aftercastle, including a helicopter landing platform aft; making structural changes in the keel plating; installing full air-conditioning for worldwide service; altering hammock slinging to full bunk sleeping; allocating dining halls and providing a higher standard of accommodation for both the naval crew and the civil scientific staff. Other major work carried out included the complete overhaul of the main propelling machinery and auxiliary engines, the installation of four very large diesel generators and the fitting of new electronic gear, radar displays and radio systems, modernized ship controls and navigational instruments, with laboratories and scientific offices, computer rooms, operations cabinets and trials equipment consoles, and facilities for both male and female personnel. Fin stabilizers and passive anti-roll tanks werg fitted to steady the ship in rough weather, making her a far more comfortable ship, both operationally and personally, in heavy seas. *Matapan* is officially stated to be the first warship to have the bulbous bow feature. All her armament was removed and she is no longer classed as a destroyer. She is joined to the 2nd Frigate Squadron, based at Portland and attached to the Underwater Weapons Establishment, but her home port is Portsmouth.

Pennant no.	D 43
Displacement	3 835 tons
Dimensions	388 × 40½ × 26 feet
Machinery	Parsons geared turbines, 2 shafts,
	shp: 50 000 = 35¾ knots designed, 30½ sea speed
Boilers	2 Admiralty three-drum type
Complement	182 ship's company
	22 scientific staff, including women
Builders	John Brown & Co. Ltd, Clydebank
Laid down	11 Mar. 1944
Launched	30 Apr. 1945
Completed	5 Sep. 1947
Reconstructed	HM Dockyard, Portsmouth, 5 Jan. 1970 to 2 Feb. 1973

MATAPAN

WHITEHEAD

This experimental vessel was a new construction job specifically intended to slot into the test and trials programme of the Navy Department of the Ministry of Defence, contrary to the former time-honoured practice of adapting or converting surplus and over-age warships or purchased small mercantile hulls for research and development projects under Admiralty control. She was designed to provide mobile preparation, firing and control facilities for weapons and research installations and is fitted with equipment for tracking weapons and targets and for analysing the results of trials. She is a ship of the recently established Royal Maritime Auxiliary Service under the jurisdiction of the Superintendent of the RMAS base at Turnchapel, Plymouth. Manned on mercantile rather than naval lines, she has, according to the latest Navy List, a Master, a Chief Officer, two second officers, a catering officer, a Chief Engineer, a second engineer, two third engineers, an electrical officer and a radio officer. She is named after Robert Whitehead, the notable torpedo development pioneer and development engineer, but before she was sponsored she was known simply as ETV 01. She has a staff of scientists in addition to the crew.

Pennant no.	A 364
Displacement	3 040 tons full load
Dimensions	319 × 48 × 17 feet
Machinery	2 Paxman diesels,
	1 shaft, bhp : 3 400 = $15\frac{1}{2}$ knots
Endurance	4 000 nautical miles at a speed of 12 knots cruising
Complement	Crew 43
	Trials and scientific staff 15
Builders	Scotts' Shipbuilding Co. Ltd, Greenock
Launched	5 May 1970
Completed	1 Feb. 1971

WHITEHEAD

CRYSTAL

Over the years, in the present century of technological progress, several ships have been referred to as 'floating test beds', but the *Crystal* is probably the only vessel thoroughly to deserve the appellation, for unlike previous so-called floating test beds, which have usually been converted or hulked obsolete fighting ships or commercial ships which had once been fitted with or still had propelling machinery, she is indeed an unpowered floating platform for sonar research and development. She is quite unique and is probably the most ungainly looking vessel ever built. Her appearance is more reminiscent of a block of office flats than a ship, although the six-storeyed high tower of truncated pyramidal shape at the end of the two-storeyed galleries extending for most of the length of the vessel is somewhat redolent of the after-castle of some futuristic galleon. She is in fact a harbour-based laboratory without self-propulsion or steering, and has to be moved by tug. She is intended to provide the Admiralty Underwater Weapons Establishment at Portland with a stable platform on which to carry out acoustic tests and other research projects. Before she was named she was a building project known as RDV 01.

Displacement	3 040 deep load
Dimensions	$413\frac{1}{2} \times 56 \times 5\frac{1}{2}$ feet
Complement	60 including scientists
Builders	HM Dockyard, Devonport
Ordered	1 Dec. 1969
Laid down	2 Mar. 1970
Completed	3 Sep. 1971

There are several other experimental trials vessels under Navy Department control:

ICEWHALE A coastal type of experimental trials vessel for the Underwater Weapons Establishment, Portland: 289 tons standard, 350 tons full load displacement, 120 feet length, 24 feet beam, 9 feet draught, speed 9 knots, complement 12.

SAREPTA Formerly the German *Frieda Peters* launched in 1920. Multi-purpose torpedo experimental, firing and recovery vessel, reclassified as TRV in 1966 and in reserve 1972: 465 tons standard displacement, 157 feet length, $27\frac{1}{2}$ feet beam, 12 feet draught, four 21-inch torpedo tubes.

WHIMBREL Formerly *NSC(E) 1012*. Experimental trials vessel of the LCT(3) tank landing craft type: 300 tons displacement, $190 \times 30 \times 4\frac{1}{2}$ feet.

CRYSTAL

RECLAIM

This unusual ship was the first deep diving and submarine rescue vessel to be built as such for the Royal Navy. Her specialized scheme of construction was based on that of the naval ocean salvage vessels of the 'King Salvor' class. She is fitted with sonar gear, radar consoles, and echo-sounding apparatus for the detection of sunken wrecks. She is also equipped for submarine rescue work. Formerly a tender to HMS *Vernon* 'stone frigate' or shore establishment, the Royal Naval Torpedo, Anti-Submarine and Diving School at Portsmouth for deep diving experiments, she was subsequently a deep diving vessel in the Portsmouth Squadron. In 1960 she was reclassified as a Mine Countermeasures Support and Diving Trials Ship and attached to the minesweeping base at Port Edgar, Scotland, known as HMS *Lochinvar*, but her mine countermeasures functions were taken over in 1968 by the new minelayer *Abdiel* and she is now listed as Diving Trials Ship. She carried out deep diving experiments off the Canary Islands in January to March 1961. She was originally allocated the name *Salverdant*.

Pennant no.	A 231
Displacement	1 200 tons standard, 1 800 tons full load
Dimensions	$218 \times 38 \times 15\frac{1}{2}$ feet
Machinery	Triple expansion steam reciprocating engines, 2 shafts, ihp: 1 500 = 12 knots
Complement	84
Builders	Wm Simons & Co. Ltd, Renfrew
Engineers	Aitchison Blair Ltd
Laid down	9 Apr. 1946
Launched	12 Mar. 1948
Completed	12 Oct. 1948

RECLAIM

BRITANNIA

This handsome vessel, one of the few ships deserving the true designation of 'ship', since she has three masts, fore, main and mizzen, was designed as a medium-sized naval hospital ship, to be used by Her Majesty The Queen in time of peace as the royal yacht to replace the quite archaic royal yacht *Victoria and Albert* built towards the end of the last century which would have been replaced by a new royal yacht under the 1939 Naval Estimates had it not been for the Second World War; in the event a new vessel was not ordered until February 1952. HMS *Britannia* has an endurance sufficient to enable her to undertake long ocean voyages of upwards of 3 000 miles at her most economical speed of 15 knots. With a modified cruiser stern and a raked bow she presents a fairly naval trim, but her construction in general originally conformed to mercantile practice. The bridge structure and funnel were built largely of aluminium alloy. The ship is fitted with Denny-Brown single fin stabilizers to reduce her roll in heavy weather from 20 degrees to six degrees. To enable her to pass under the bridges of the St Lawrence Seaway when she visited Canada the top 20 feet of her mainmast and the radio aerial on her foremast were hinged in November 1958 so that they could be lowered as required. Between 2 October 1972 and 6 July 1973 she underwent her first major refit after nearly 20 years of service as a royal yacht and as a 'stand-in' for a warship during fleet exercises. The crew's quarters were rehabilitated with bunk beds instead of obsolete hammock slinging, and air-conditioning was installed. Larger generators for more electrical power were fitted, and all mechanical and electrical equipment was overhauled or replaced, the ship's manually operated telephone switchboard being replaced by an automatic exchange.

Pennant no.	A00 ·
Displacement	4 000 tons standard, 5 111 tons full load
Measurement	5 769 tons gross before refit
Dimensions	$412\frac{1}{2} \times 55 \times 17$ feet
Machinery	Single reduction geared steam turbines, 2 shafts, shp : 12 000 = 21 knots continuous cruising ($22\frac{3}{4}$ knots on trials)
Boilers	2
Complement	270 original accommodation, now reduced
Builders	John Brown & Co. Ltd, Clydebank
Laid down	16 June 1952
Launched	16 Apr. 1953
Completed	14 Jan. 1954

BRITANNIA

Official

HECATE   HECLA   HYDRA

New dual purpose deep ocean survey ships for the Royal Navy, the first to be designed with a combined oceanographical and hydrographical role and the first to be built on commercial lines without a supplementary naval function. Of merchant ship design, and similar in many respects to the Royal Research Ship *Discovery,* they have range and endurance to fit them for their specialized work. The hull is strengthened for navigation in ice, and a propeller is built into a transverse tunnel in the bow for better manoeuvrability. The ships are each equipped with a helicopter hangar and adjacent flight deck aft, chartroom, drawing office, photographic studio, two laboratories and electrical, engineering and shipwright workshops.

Displacement	2 733 tons full load
Measurement	2 898 tons gross
Dimensions	260 × 49 × 15 feet
Aircraft	1 Wasp helicopter
Machinery	Diesel electric, 1 shaft,
	3 Davey Paxman Ventura turbo charged diesels, bhp : 3 840
	1 electric motor, shp : 2 000 = 14 knots
Complement	118 (accommodation for 123)

	No.	Builders	Laid down	Launched	Completed
Hecate	A 137	Yarrow & Co. Ltd, Scotstoun	26 Oct. 1964	31 Mar. 1965	20 Dec. 1965
Hecla	A 133	Yarrow, Scotstoun and Blythswood	6 May 1964	21 Dec. 1964	9 Sep. 1965
Hydra	A 144	Yarrow, Scotstoun and Blythswood	14 Aug. 1964	14 July 1965	5 May 1966

HERALD

A later version of the 'Hecla' class design, varying slightly in particulars commenced in February 1972 by Robb Caledon, Leith, was launched on 4 October 1973.

(The surveying ship *Vidal,* A 200, of Admiralty design, 2 200 tons full load displacement, completed at HM Dockyard, Chatham, in 1954, was officially placed on the sales list in 1972 but was still at Chatham in April 1973.)

HYDRA and HECLA *Official*

BEAGLE   BULLDOG   FAWN   FOX

These very good-looking ships, built to commercial standards and designed for maximum habitability, constitute a class of coastal survey ships for the charting of shallow waters, and are capable of hydrographic survey anywhere in the world. Intended for duty overseas, working in pairs, they are classed as 100 A1 at Lloyd's and additionally to naval standards where applicable. Each ship is fitted with a passive tank stabilizer to reduce rolling, the most modern echo sounders, precision ranging radar, Decca 'Hifix' system and automatic steering. All four ships are air-conditioned throughout. Each carries a 28½-foot survey motor launch in davits. *Fawn* and *Fox* replaced the 'Ton' class coastal minesweeper conversions *Mermaid* (formerly *Sullington*) and *Myrmidon* (ex-*Edderton*). The names originally allocated to this class were *Albacore, Albatross, Barracouta, Bulldog, Fawn* and *Fox*, but these were changed in 1965 to *Beagle, Bulldog, Fawn, Fox, Pelican* and *Porcupine*, and the two last were cancelled in 1967. *Bulldog* was the first of the class to be commissioned, on 21 March 1968, and the other three were commissioned by the end of the year.

Displacement	800 tons standard, 1 088 tons full load
Dimensions	189 × 37½ × 12 feet
Machinery	4 Lister Blackstone 8 cylinder 4 stroke diesels coupled to 2 shafts, bhp : 2 000 = 15 knots maximum designed. Controllable pitch propellers
Complement	38

	No.	Builders	Laid down	Launched	Completed
Beagle	A 319	Brooke Marine Ltd, Lowestoft	15 Nov. 1966	7 Sep. 1967	23 Mar. 1968
Bulldog	A 317	Brooke Marine Ltd, Lowestoft	15 Nov. 1966	12 July 1967	9 May 1968
Fawn	A 335	Brooke Marine Ltd, Lowestoft	21 Dec. 1966	29 Feb. 1968	3 Oct. 1968
Fox	A 320	Brooke Marine Ltd, Lowestoft	21 Dec. 1966	6 Nov. 1967	11 July 1968

BULLDOG *Official*

ECHO

EGERIA

ENTERPRISE

The first Inshore Survey Craft, HMS *Echo,* was built by J. Samuel White & Co. Ltd, Cowes, Isle of Wight, launched on 1 May 1957 and commissioned on 12 September 1958, her main propelling machinery having been manufactured by Davey Paxman & Co. Ltd, Colchester. She was of all wooden construction with glued laminated members. In peacetime she has no armament but she was initially and experimentally fitted with a 40-mm gun for her first trials, and she retains her seat for the gun mounting. In wartime she could be used as an armed inshore minehunter, the type on which her design was based. Basically she conforms to the pattern of the inshore minesweepers of the 'Ley' class, but she was specifically intended for coastal and harbour hydrographic surveying duties around the British Isles, and she has the ability to navigate in shoal water, to obtain and log depths and detect wrecks on the sea bed, and to fix the position with accuracy. She is equipped with two echo sounding machines and sonar for wreck location, and survey equipment for triangulation ashore. She was provided with modern radar, wire sweep gear, echo sounding launch and a modern chart room. *Egeria* was built by Wm Weatherhead & Sons Ltd, Cockenzie, and *Enterprise* by M. W. Blackmore & Sons Ltd, Bideford.

Pennant nos.	*Echo* A 70, *Egeria* A 72, *Enterprise* A 71
Displacement	120 tons standard, 160 tons full load
Dimensions	$107 \times 22 \times 6\frac{3}{4}$ feet
Machinery	2 Paxman diesels, 2 shafts. Controllable pitch propellers.
	bhp : 700 = 14 knots maximum, 12 knots normal speed
Complement	18, but accommodation for 22

There are two other inshore survey craft :
WATERWITCH M 272 (ex-*Powderham* M 2720) and **WOODLARK** M 2780 (ex-*Yaxham*), both former inshore mine-sweepers of the 'Ham' class (see previous page) converted to replace the old survey motor launches *Meda* and *Medusa* for operations in inshore waters at home. *Waterwitch*, pennant number latterly M 304, was seconded to the Port Auxiliary Service in 1968. Particulars of both ships : 120 tons standard, 160 tons full load displacement ; $107\frac{1}{2}$ feet length, 22 feet beam, $5\frac{1}{2}$ feet draught ; diesels of 1 100 brake horse power turning 2 shafts = 14 knots ; complement 18.

ENTERPRISE

ENGADINE

Strictly speaking this unique ship is a Royal Fleet Auxiliary and not one of HM ships in the Royal Navy, but she is more navy-orientated than most other vessels of the Royal Fleet Auxiliary Service. Projected under the 1964–65 Navy Estimates, she was ordered on 18 August 1964. She was sponsored in a very unusual way, having been officially named on 15 September 1966 when high winds caused the postponement of the launching ceremony until 16 September. She was accepted into service on 15 December 1967. She was then the largest ship to have been built by the company. She was designed with the intention of training helicopter crews in deep water operations against submarines. She is fitted with Denny Brown stabilizers to provide greater ship control during helicopter operations and she is the only Royal Fleet Auxiliary Service vessel so equipped. Considering her very specialized role she is a handsome-looking ship despite the flight deck aft and the square control drome amidships with its look-out tower running in continuity with the bridge superstructure. With increased speed and without undue enlargement of dimensions such a ship might well be envisaged as the precursor of a type of small carrier of V/STOL aircraft, a design lending itself to mass production in emergency.

Pennant no.	K 08
Displacement	8 000 tons standard, 9 000 tons full load
Measurement	6 384 tons gross, 2 848 tons net
Dimensions	$424 \times 58\frac{1}{2} \times 22\frac{1}{4}$ feet
Aircraft	4 Wessex and 2 Wasp or 2 Sea King helicopters
Machinery	1 Sulzer 5 cylinder 2 stroke turbo charged diesel, bhp : 5 500 = 16 knots
Complement	61 (Royal Fleet Auxiliary Service) and 14 (Royal Navy) (accommodation for a further 113 officers and ratings of the Royal Navy)
Builders	Henry Robb Ltd, Leith
Ordered	18 Aug. 1964
Laid down	9 Aug. 1965
Launched	16 Sep. 1966
Completed	15 Dec. 1967

(The helicopter support ship *Lofoten,* converted LST(3) 3027, is laid up.)

ENGADINE

LYNESS   STROMNESS   TARBATNESS

Considering their multi-purpose role as ships of the Royal Fleet Auxiliary Service especially intended for the support of fighting ships of the Royal Navy, these vessels are good-looking and fairly symmetrical. All ordered on 7 December 1964, they were designed and built by Swan Hunter & Wigham Richardson Ltd, Wallsend-on-Tyne, to meet specific naval require-ments. They are installed with Sulzer type remotely controlled main propelling machinery, and auxiliary machinery manu-factured by Wallsend Slipway & Engineering Co. Ltd. Lifts and mobile appliances are provided for handling stores internally and there is a new replenishment at sea system and a helicopter landing platform for transferring loads at sea. A novel feature of these ships is the use of closed-circuit television to monitor the movement of stores. All three vessels are air-conditioned in living and working spaces for operating in tropical or otherwise intemperate climates. *Lyness* is listed as an Air Store Support Ship in the Navy List and her two sister ships as Stores Support Ships.

Displacement	16 500 tons laden, official approximate figure
Measurement	12 359 to 14 113 tons gross, 4 744 tons net, 7 782 tons deadweight
Dimensions	524 × 72 × 25½ feet
Aircraft	Facilities for 2 helicopters
Machinery	Wallsend-Sulzer 8-cylinder diesels, bhp: 11 520 = 17 knots
Complement	Upwards of 104 Accommodation for 184

	No.	Builders	Ordered	Launched	Completed
Lyness	A 339	Swan, Hunter, Wallsend	7 Dec. 1964	7 Apr. 1966	22 Dec. 1966
Stromness	A 344	Swan, Hunter, Wallsend	7 Dec. 1964	16 Sep. 1966	21 Mar. 1967
Tarbatness	A 345	Swan, Hunter, Wallsend	7 Dec. 1964	27 Feb. 1967	27 Sep. 1967

TARBATNESS *Official*

REGENT   RESOURCE

With funnel aft these vessels have the appearance of fleet replenishment tankers rather than stores supply ships, and in this respect differ from the other three fleet support ships with 'Re' names, *Reliant, Resurgent* and *Retainer,* which are quite symmetrical with funnel almost dead amidships. Both were ordered on 24 January 1963 but from different builders in different countries, although they are practically identical. With their replenishment services they enable the Fleet to operate at maximum efficiency in all parts of the world and to remain independent of shore facilities for extended periods. They have lifts for armaments and stores and are provided with helicopter platforms for transferring loads to and from warships at sea. Both ships were designed from the outset as Fleet Replenishment Ships in contrast to previous naval supply ships which had been converted merchant vessels. They are air-conditioned throughout for service in hot or cold regions. Their official title was formerly Ammunition, Food, Explosives and Stores Ships, but they are now shown in the Navy List as Fleet Replenishment Ships.

Displacement	19 000 tons full load, deep departure
Measurement	19 100 and 18 029 tons gross, respectively
Dimensions	$640 \times 77\frac{1}{4} \times 26\frac{1}{4}$ feet
Aircraft	1 Wessex helicopter
Guns	Two 40-mm Bofors, single
Machinery	AEI geared steam turbines, 1 shaft, shp : 20 000 = 20 knots
Complement	119 Royal Fleet Auxiliary Service and Merchant Navy, 52 Ministry of Defence Navy Department civil servants, 11 Royal Navy for helicopter flying and maintenance

	No.	Builders	Ordered	Launched	Completed
Regent	A 486	Harland & Wolff Ltd, Belfast	24 Jan. 1963	9 Mar. 1966	31 Dec. 1966
Resource	A 480	Scotts' SB & Eng. Co. Greenock	24 Jan. 1963	11 Feb. 1966	31 Dec. 1966

REGENT

RELIANT

This handsome-looking ship with funnel and light mast amidships, central bridge and superstructure and evenly distributed king-posts, two forward and two aft, was originally a mercantile grain carrier which traded for two years, working between the Gulf of Mexico and the United Kingdom, before being purchased from the Ropner Shipping Company. She was converted for her new role as a vessel of the Royal Fleet Auxiliary Service at North Shields, and sailed from HM Dockyard, Chatham, on 4 November 1958 destined for the Far East as the Royal Navy's first air victualling stores issuing ship capable of replenishing aircraft carriers at sea. Her conversion was based on the concept that aircraft carriers should be able to spend more time at sea and be independent of shore bases. She has six holds and was fitted with the latest automatic tensioning winch for the transfer of stores to aircraft carriers, commando carriers and other amphibious ships in unfavourable weather. When refitted she was provided with a helicopter landing platform built over the poop deckhouse with netting surrounds. She can carry some 40 000 different patterns of aircraft spares and general naval stores. Her living and operating spaces are fully air-conditioned for service in the tropics, and she has an endurance of 50 days' steaming at a service speed of 16 knots. She was originally named *Somersby*, but was renamed *Reliant* in 1958. She is specifically an Air Stores Support Ship.

Pennant no.	A 84
Displacement	4 447 tons light as built, 13 737 tons full load
Measurement	9 290 tons deadweight—summer, 8 460 tons gross
Dimensions	$468\frac{3}{4} \times 61\frac{1}{2} \times 26\frac{1}{4}$ feet
Machinery	Doxford 6-cylinder diesels, 1 shaft, bhp : 8 250 = 18 knots
Aircraft	Facilities for helicopter aft
Complement	102 to 110
Builders	Sir James Laing & Sons Ltd, Sunderland
Engineers	Hawthorn Leslie (Engineers) Ltd, Hebburn-on-Tyne
Launched	9 Sep. 1963
Completed	1954
Converted	North Shields, 1958

RELIANT *Official*

RESURGENT   RETAINER

These ships have a distinctive appearance with a somewhat low-lying hull, funnel amidships, lengthy but shallow super-structure, and equidistant masts forward and aft. They were formerly passenger and cargo motor vessels, both built for the China Navigation Company by Scotts' Shipbuilding and Engineering Company, Greenock, and completed in 1950 and 1951 respectively, and they still look more like mercantile vessels than naval auxiliary ships. The *Retainer* was formerly a passenger and cargo liner trading along the coast of China. She was purchased in 1952 and converted into a naval stores ship during autumn 1954 to April 1955 by Palmers Hebburn Co. Ltd, where further conversion work was carried out from March to August 1957 to extend her facilities as a stores ship, including the fitting out of holds to carry naval stores, the installation of lifts for loads, the provision of extra cargo handling gear and new bridge wings. The *Resurgent* was taken over on completion for employment as a fleet replenishment ship. A landing platform for a helicopter was built on aft. The official title for both ships was originally Store Support Ships, but latterly they have been known more specifically as Armament Support Ships, although the latest Navy List shows them under the Royal Fleet Auxiliary Service as Fleet Replenishment Ships. The name originally allocated to *Resurgent* was *Changchow*, and *Retainer* formerly bore the name *Chungking*.

Pennant nos.	*Resurgent* A 280, *Retainer* A 329
Displacement	14 000 tons normal load, official estimate
Measurement	*Resurgent:* 9 511 tons gross
	Retainer: 9 301 to 9 355 tons gross
Dimensions	$477\frac{1}{4} \times 62 \times 29$ feet
Aircraft	Platform aft for helicopter
Machinery	Doxford diesel engine, 1 shaft,
	bhp : 6 500 = 15 knots
Complement	107
Builders	Scotts' Shipbuilding & Engineering Co. Ltd, Greenock
Launched	1951 and 1950 respectively
Completed	*Resurgent* 1951, *Retainer* 1950
Purchased	*Resurgent* 1951, *Retainer* 1952
Converted	*Retainer:* autumn 1954 to April 1955 and
	Mar. 1957 to Aug. 1957 by Palmers Hebburn Co. Ltd

RETAINER *Official*

BACCHUS

HEBE

Among the support ships which keep the fighting Fleet supplied by replenishing shore bases at which warships call are these two smaller vessels of the Royal Fleet Auxiliary Service which are listed in the Navy List as store carriers, though they are technically rated as dry cargo ships. They were originally built as freighters for the British India Steam Navigation Company but were taken over by the Royal Navy on completion on a long term bare boat charter and operated as Royal Fleet Auxiliaries. A feature of their construction is that their main propelling machinery and the accommodation for their officers and ratings are right aft as is the normal case in oil tankers. They spend most of their lives making the passage back and forth between the Far East or other overseas areas and their home ports. They carry 720 tons of fuel for their own use in their oil engines.

Pennant nos.	*Bacchus:* A 404
	Hebe: A 406
Displacement	2 740 tons light, 7 958 tons full load
Measurement	4 823 tons gross, 2 441 tons net, 5 218 tons deadweight
Dimensions	379 × 55 × 22 feet
Machinery	Swan Hunter Sulzer diesel,
	1 shaft, bhp : 5 500 = 15 knots
Complement	57
Builders	Henry Robb Ltd, Leith
Completed	*Bacchus:* Sep. 1962
	Hebe: May 1962

'Fort' Class: The armament support ships *Fort Rosalie,* A 186, and *Fort Sandusky,* A 316, although still in the most recently published Navy List, were scheduled for return to the Canadian Government in 1972. They were similar in type to the maintenance ships of the 'Mull' and 'Head' classes, see page 90. Of their sister ships *Fort Beauharnois* was scrapped in 1962, *Fort Constantine* was broken up at Hamburg in 1969, *Fort Charlotte* was sold in 1968, *Fort Duquesne* was broken up in Holland in 1967, *Fort Dunvegan* in 1969. *Fort Langley* was returned to the Canadian Government and arrived at Bilbao, Spain, to be broken up on 21 July 1970.

HEBE *Official*

GOLD ROVER GREEN ROVER GREY ROVER BLUE ROVER BLACK ROVER

Although there is a gap of some four years between the construction of the *Gold Rover,* about to be outfitted at the time of writing, and the other three ships, they are all of the same 'Rover' class designed to replenish HM ships at sea with fuel, fresh water, limited dry cargo and refrigerated stores in all areas of the world and under all conditions whilst under way. A feature of the appearance of these ships is the superstructure about one third the distance of the ship from the stern, the cluster of bridge, mast, raked back and streamlined mast, and control tower piling up into a pyramid and then levelling off aft into the flight deck raised above the counter. The relatively extensive helicopter landing platform thus provided is served by a special goods lift to enable stores to be transferred at sea by helicopter. The main engines and single four-bladed controllable pitch propeller can be operated directly from the bridge or from a noise-insulated and air-conditioned compartment within the engine room. A bow transverse thrust unit is fitted to make manoeuvring easier in harbour and confined waterways. The accommodation includes cafeteria messing, a cinema and a recreation and hobby room. The vessels are air-conditioned for service in both tropical and Arctic climates. All are classed as Royal Fleet Auxiliaries, but according to the Navy List *Blue Rover* is a Fleet Replenishment Tanker while *Green Rover* and *Grey Rover* are listed as small fleet tankers.

Displacement	11 522 tons full load
Measurement	3 185 tons net, 7 060 tons deadweight, 7 510 tons gross
Dimensions	461 × 63 × 24 feet
Machinery	*Black Rover, Gold Rover:* 2 Pielstick 16-cylinder medium speed diesels.
	Other three: 2 Ruston & Hornsby 16-cyl. uni-directional,
	1 shaft, bhp: 16 000 = 19 knots
Complement	*Black Rover, Gold Rover:* 47
	Other three: 42

	No.	Builders	Launched
Gold Rover	A 271	Swan, Hunter Shipbuilders, Neptune Yard, Wallsend	7 Mar. 1973
Green Rover	A 268	Swan, Hunter Shipbuilders Ltd, Hebburn-on-Tyne	18 Dec. 1968
Grey Rover	A 269	Swan, Hunter Shipbuilders Ltd, Hebburn-on-Tyne	17 Apr. 1969
Blue Rover	A 270	Swan, Hunter Shipbuilders Ltd, Hebburn-on-Tyne	11 Nov. 1969
Black Rover	A 272	Swan, Hunter Shipbuilders, Neptune Yard, Wallsend	30 Aug. 1973

GREY ROVER

DERWENTDALE   DEWDALE

These are by far the largest fleet oilers in the Royal Navy. It was announced on 13 July 1967 that the Navy Department of the Ministry of Defence had officially chartered three large tankers for service East of Suez, and renamed them, reintroducing traditional 'Dale' class names. After limited modifications the three ships operated in the Indian Ocean area. But *Ennerdale* sank on 1 June 1970 after striking a submerged hazard in the Indian Ocean. Her particulars were: Measurement: 16 255 tons net, 30 112 tons gross, 47 250 tons deadweight; Dimensions: $710 \times 98\frac{1}{2} \times 37\frac{1}{2}$ feet; Machinery: B. & W. 8-cylinder diesels, 1 shaft, 16 800 bhp = $15\frac{1}{2}$ knots; Complement 51. *Ennerdale* was formerly the MV *Naess Scotsman*; *Derwentdale* was formerly the MV *Halcyon Breeze*; and *Dewdale* was formerly the *Edenfield*. Although the three ships had common suffix 'dale' names it will be observed from the foregoing and the data of the other two ships below that they were in no wise sister ships like the other classes of fleet oilers. *Ennerdale* was built by Kieler Howaldstwerke for commercial usage and launched on 31 August 1963. *Derwentdale* was a commercial oil tanker built by Hitachi, Japan, and launched on 8 January 1964, taken over by Great Britain in 1967 and chartered from the Court Line. *Dewdale* was built by Harland & Wolff Ltd, Belfast, for mercantile freighting and launched on 5 March 1965. The two ships are manned by Royal Fleet Auxiliary Service personnel from the Merchant Navy and wear the Blue Ensign. They were formerly officially rated as Mobile Bulk Tankers but are now in the Navy List as Mobile Reserve Tankers. Pennant numbers: *Derwentdale* A 221; *Dewdale* A 219.

Derwentdale

Displacement	88 555 tons full load
Measurement	28 288 tons net, 42 343 tons gross, 72 550 tons deadweight
Dimensions	$799 \times 117\frac{3}{4} \times 42\frac{1}{3}$ feet
Machinery	Burmeister & Wain 9-cylinder diesels, I shaft, bhp: 20 700 = $15\frac{1}{2}$ knots
Complement	58

Dewdale

Displacement	81 953 tons full load
Measurement	21 542 tons net; 35 805 tons gross; 63 588 tons deadweight
Dimensions	$774\frac{1}{2} \times 108 \times 41\frac{1}{2}$ feet
Machinery	Burmeister & Wain 9-cylinder diesels, 1 shaft, bhp: 17 000 = 15 knots
Complement	56

DERWENTDALE *Official*

OLMEDA (*ex-Oleander*)   OLNA   OLWEN (*ex-Olynthus*)

A novel class of tankers design by Hawthorn Leslie and Swan, Hunter to meet specific naval requirements. Intended for the support of the Fleet, with handling gear for transferring fuels and stores by jackstay and derricks while steaming at speed. Right aft a helicopter landing platform and hangar enable warships to collect stores by air. These ships have sophisticated propelling machinery control systems, including bridge control of ahead revolutions, and are specially strengthened for operations in ice. The accommodation is of a high standard and fully air-conditioned. When they joined the Royal Fleet Auxiliary Service these oilers, listed as large fleet tankers in the Navy List, were the largest and fastest RFA ships. *Olna* has a transverse bow thrust unit for improved manoeuvrability in confined waters, and a new design of replenishment at sea system. *Olwen*, originally named *Olynthus*, was renamed in September 1967 to avoid confusion with the submarine *Olympus* in correspondence and by telephone, and *Olmeda*, first named *Oleander*, was renamed to obviate confusion with the frigate *Leander*. *Olna* and *Olwen* were engined by Hawthorn Leslie (Engineers) Ltd while *Olmeda* was powered by Wallsend Slipway & Eng. Co. Ltd.

Displacement	10 890 tons light, 33 240 tons full load
Measurement	22 350 tons deadweight, 18 600 tons gross
Dimensions	648 × 84 × 34 feet
Aircraft	2 Wessex helicopters (can carry 3)
Machinery	Pametrada double reduction geared turbines, bhp: 26 500 = 19 knots ($21\frac{1}{4}$ knots on trials)
Boilers	2 Babcock & Wilcox
Complement	87

	No.	Builders	Launched	Completed
Olmeda	A 124	Swan, Hunter Ltd, Wallsend-on-Tyne	19 Nov. 1964	18 Oct. 1965
Olna	A 123	Hawthorn Leslie Ltd, Hebburn-on-Tyne	28 July 1965	1 Apr. 1966
Olwen	A 122	Hawthorn Leslie Ltd, Hebburn-on-Tyne	10 July 1964	21 June 1965

OLNA

TIDEFLOW TIDEPOOL TIDEREACH TIDESPRING TIDESURGE

The *Tidereach* was the first of the then new Fleet Replenishment Tankers, having been specially designed for the support of the Fleet and the replenishment of warships while under way at sea. With 15 000 tons of fuel oil cargo they are capacious and fitted with modern handling gear for transferring food, stores, ammunition, oil and jet aircraft fuels by jackstay and derricks. Oil cargo can be discharged at a high rate to ships on either beam or astern while steaming at speed. The sister ships of *Tidereach* are *Tideflow*, originally named *Tiderace,* and *Tidesurge,* renamed from *Tiderange* in 1958. A fourth ship of this original group, the *Tide Austral,* was renamed *Supply* on 7 September 1962. These are only technically different from the two ships built eight years later, *Tidespring* and *Tidepool.* This pair are highly specialized ships for fuelling and storing naval vessels at sea and capable of high performance under rigorous service conditions. With a capacity of 13 000 tons of cargo fuel, their all-round capability is enhanced by the incorporation of a helicopter platform and hangar.

Displacement	8 531 tons light, 25 931 tons full load (1963 ships)
	9 040 tons light, 25 940 tons full load (earlier ships)
Measurement	17 400 tons deadweight, 14 130 tons gross (1963 ships)
	16 900 tons deadweight, 13 700 tons gross (early ships)
Dimensions	583 × 71 × 32 feet
Machinery	Double reduction geared turbines, shp : 15 000 = 17 knots
Boilers	2 Babcock & Wilcox
Complement	115

	No.	Builders	Laid down	Launched	Completed
Tideflow	A 97	Sir James Laing, Sunderland	30 Aug. 1953	30 Aug. 1954	25 Jan. 1956
Tidepool	A 76	Hawthorn Leslie, Hebburn	4 Dec. 1961	11 Dec. 1962	28 June 1963
Tidereach	A 96	Swan, Hunter, Wallsend, Tyne	2 June 1953	2 June 1954	30 Aug. 1955
Tidespring	A 75	Hawthorn Leslie, Hebburn	24 July 1961	3 May 1962	18 Jan. 1963
Tidesurge	A 98	Thompson & Sons, Sunderland	1 July 1953	1 July 1954	30 Aug. 1955

TIDESPRING

BAYLEAF BRAMBLELEAF CHERRYLEAF ORANGELEAF PEARLEAF

These vessels constituting the 'Leaf' class are officially designated as support tankers in the Royal Fleet Auxiliary Service. *Bayleaf* (ex-*London Integrity*) and *Brambleleaf* (ex-*London Loyalty*) were both acquired from London & Overseas Freighters Ltd on 22 May 1959. *Orangeleaf* (ex-MV *Southern Satellite*) was acquired from South Georgi Co. Ltd on 25 May 1959. *Pearleaf* was built for Jacobs and Partners Ltd, London, and chartered by the Royal Navy on completion : she can carry three different grades of cargo. All 'Leaf' class tankers have astern fuelling capabilities. *Pearleaf* and *Plumleaf* also have abeam fuelling capabilities. The oiler *Cherryleaf*, A 82 (ex-MV *Laurelwood*), was returned to her original owners, Molasses & General Transport Co. Ltd, in 1966 and sold to Greek interests. The oiler *Appleleaf*, A 83 (ex-MV *George Lyras*), the first of the 'Leaf' group acquired by the Royal Navy, taken over in 1959, was returned to her original owners in January 1970. *Plumleaf* was reported returned and renamed *Mayfair Loyalty* in June 1972. *Cherryleaf* reappeared in the Navy List in March 1973. (She was formerly *Overseas Adventurer;* she carries the same pennant number as the previous *Cherryleaf*.)

Bayleaf and *Brambleleaf*:	Measurement	17 960 tons deadweight, 12 123 tons gross, 7 042 tons net
	Dimensions	$556\frac{3}{4} \times 71\frac{1}{3} \times 30$ feet
	Machinery	Doxford 6-cylinder diesel, bhp : 6 800 = $14\frac{1}{2}$ knots
Cherryleaf:	Measurement	19 770 tons deadweight, 13 721 tons gross, 7 648 tons net
	Dimensions	$559\frac{1}{2} \times 72 \times 30\frac{3}{4}$ feet
	Machinery	Doxford 6-cylinder diesel, bhp : 8 400 = $14\frac{1}{2}$ knots
Orangeleaf:	Measurement	17 475 tons deadweight, 12 481 tons gross, 6 949 tons net
	Dimensions	$556\frac{1}{2} \times 71\frac{1}{4} \times 30\frac{1}{2}$ feet
	Machinery	Doxford 6-cylinder diesel, bhp : 6 800 = 15 knots
Pearleaf:	Displacement	24 900 tons full load
	Measurement	18 045 tons deadweight, 12 139 tons gross, 7 216 tons net
	Dimensions	$568 \times 71\frac{3}{4} \times 30$ feet
	Machinery	Rowan Doxford 6-cylinder diesels, bhp : 8 880 = $15\frac{3}{4}$ knots
Plumleaf:	Displacement	24 920 tons full load
	Measurement	18 562 tons deadweight, 12 692 tons gross
	Dimensions	$560 \times 72 \times 30$ feet
	Machinery	N.E. Doxford 6-cylinder diesels, bhp : 9 350 = $15\frac{1}{2}$ knots

	No.	Builders	Launched	Completed
Bayleaf	A 79	Furness Shipbuilding Co. Ltd, Haverton, Tees	28 Oct. 1954	28 Apr. 1955
Brambleleaf	A 81	Furness Shipbuilding Co. Ltd, Haverton, Tees	10 June 1953	10 Jan. 1954
Cherryleaf	A 82	Rheinstahl Nordseewerte, Emden	1962	Feb. 1963
Orangeleaf	A 80	Furness Shipbuilding Co. Ltd, Haverton, Tees	8 Feb. 1955	8 June 1955
Pearleaf	A 77	Blythswood Shipbuilding Co. Ltd, Scotstoun	15 Oct. 1959	15 Jan. 1960
Plumleaf	A 78	Blyth Drydock & Engineering Co. Ltd	29 Mar. 1960	29 July 1960

PEARLEAF *Official*

WAVE BARON   WAVE CHIEF   WAVE PRINCE   WAVE RULER

These four ships are the survivors of a practically uniform group of no fewer than twenty fleet oilers known as the 'Wave' class, most of which have been disposed of in recent years, and these last representatives of a type so well known by the Royal Navy since the Second World War will themselves not last much longer; indeed only two were shown as active and manned in a recent Navy List, for they have given yeoman service for over a quarter of a century and are being replaced by more modern vessels. All are classed as ships of the Royal Fleet Auxiliary Service, but latterly and more specifically *Wave Chief* was officially listed as a Large Fleet Tanker, *Wave Baron* as a Fleet Replenishment Tanker, *Wave Prince* as a freighter, while *Wave Ruler* was acting as the oiling depot ship at Gan, the island staging base in the Indian Ocean, replacing *Wave Victor* which has been sold for scrap. Of the remainder of the class *Wave Commander* and *Wave Liberator* were scrapped in 1959. *Wave Conqueror* and *Wave King* were sold in 1960. *Wave Emperor, Wave Governor, Wave Premier* and *Wave Regent* were scrapped in 1960. *Wave Monarch* was sold to foreign interests in 1961. *Wave Protector* was broken up in Italy in 1963. *Wave Knight* was broken up at Antwerp in 1964. *Wave Master* was scrapped in 1964. *Wave Sovereign* was sold in 1967. *Wave Duke* and *Wave Laird* were sold for scrap in 1970.

Displacement	4 750 tons light, 8 200 tons standard, 16 650 tons full load
Measurement	11 900 tons deadweight, 8 447 to 8 350 tons gross
Dimensions	$492\frac{1}{2} \times 64\frac{1}{2} \times 28\frac{1}{2}$ feet
Machinery	Double reduction geared turbines, Metrovik in *Wave Baron* and *Wave Chief*, Parsons in *Wave Prince* and *Wave Ruler*. shp : 6 800 = $14\frac{1}{2}$ knots
Boilers	Three-drum type
Complement	60

	No.	Builders	Launched
Wave Baron (ex-*Empire Flodden*)	A 242	Furness SB Co. Ltd, Haverton Hill	19 Feb. 1946
Wave Chief (ex-*Empire Edgehill*)	A 265	Harland & Wolff Ltd, Govan, Glasgow	4 Apr. 1946
Wave Prince (ex-*Empire Herald*)	A 207	Sir James Laing & Sons, Sunderland	27 July 1945
Wave Ruler (ex-*Empire Evesham*)	A 212	Furness SB, Haverton Hill-on-Tees	17 Jan. 1946

WAVE CHIEF

Official

BLACK RANGER   BROWN RANGER   GOLD RANGER

Formerly designated fleet attendant tankers, these ships are included under Royal Fleet Auxiliary Service vessels in the Navy List as small fleet tankers. They are all fitted with a special derrick on the beam to facilitate fuelling at sea. The funnel is on the port side aft. Of their sister ships *Gray Ranger* was lost during the Second World War, *Green Ranger* was deleted from the list in 1965, and *Blue Ranger,* in reserve, was on the disposal list in 1972. *Gold Ranger* was still in the most recently published Navy List, but the 'Gold' prefix has been given to a new tanker of the 'Rover' class and she will be discarded.

Pennant nos.	A 163, A 169, A 130, respectively
Displacement	6 630 tons full load
Measurement	3 313 to 3 417 tons gross, 3 435 to 3 788 tons deadweight
Dimensions	365¾ (*Gold Ranger* 355½) × 47 × 20 feet
Machinery	Burmeister & Wain diesels, bhp : 2 750 = 12 knots
Builders	Harland & Wolff Ltd, Glasgow (*Gold Ranger* Caledon SB & Eng. Co. Ltd, Dundee)
Launched	22 Aug. 1940 (*Bl.R.*), 12 Dec. 1940(*Br.R.*), 12 Mar. 1941(*G.R.*)

EDDYFIRTH A 261

Sole survivor of the 'Eddy' class. Royal Fleet Auxiliary officially listed as a coastal tanker. Displacement : 1 960 tons light, 4 160 tons full load. Measurement : 2 300 tons gross, 2 200 tons deadweight. Dimensions : 286 × 44 × 17¼. Machinery : 1 set triple expansion, 1 shaft, 1 750 ihp = 12 knots. Boilers : 2 oil burning cylindrical. Built by Lobnitz & Co. Ltd, Renfrew. Launched on 10 September 1953, completed on 10 February 1954. Constructed on the combined transverse and longitudinal system of framing and classed 100 A1 at Lloyd's for the carriage of petroleum in bulk. Cargo capacity : 1 650 tons oil. Of her sisters, *Eddybay, Eddybeach, Eddycliffe, Eddycreek* and *Eddyreef* were disposed of in 1963–64, *Eddyrock* was sold in 1967 and *Eddyness* was sold for scrapping in 1970.
Later small '0' Class: Rowanol (ex-*Cedarol,* ex-*Ebonol*) A 284, last of this port oiler type, was sold in 1972. Her three sisters, *Birchol, Oakol* and *Teakol,* were sold in 1969.

OILBIRD   OILFIELD   OILMAN   OILPRESS   OILSTONE   OILWELL

These small vessels were designed as coastal tankers but are classified as yard oilers with Y pennant numbers. Three are employed as diesel oil carriers and three as furnace fuel oil carriers. All were ordered on 10 May 1967 from Appledore Shipbuilders Ltd, Devon, and launched in 1968 and 1969.

Pennant nos.	Y 25, Y 24, Y 26, Y 21, Y 22, and Y 23 respectively
Displacement	280 tons standard, 530 tons full load
Measurement	250 tons gross
Dimensions	139½ × 30 × 8⅓ feet
Machinery	1 Lister Blackstone diesel, 1 shaft, bhp : 400 = 10 knots
Complement	11

BLACK RANGER

GOLDENEYE GARGANEY GOOSANDER MANDARIN PINTAIL POCHARD

The *Mandarin* was the first of a new class of marine service multi-purpose vessels specifically designed and constructed to be employed for mooring, salvage, and boom work. Previously these several tasks had been separately undertaken by specialist vessels such as the mooring vessels of the 'Moor' class, the salvage vessels of the 'Salv' class and the boom defence or bar vessels of the 'Bar' class, but this newly evolved type was able to perform all three services. They are capable of laying out and servicing the heaviest moorings used by ships of the Royal Navy and also of maintaining booms for harbour defence. Their heavy lifting equipment enables a wide range of salvage operations to be undertaken, especially in clearance work of harbours and port approaches. The special heavy winches installed have an ability for tidal lifts of upwards of 200 tons over the apron. The *Mandarin* and *Pintail* are a pair constituting the earlier 'Wild Duck' class with an original scheme of complement providing accommodation for a naval crew of 24, while the *Garganey* and *Goldeneye* are the second pair known as the Later 'Wild Duck' class intended for civilian manning with a crew of 25 for port auxiliary service. The *Mandarin,* handed over from her builders on 5 March 1964, and *Garganey,* accepted into naval jurisdiction in 1966, are now shown in the Navy List under the Royal Maritime Auxiliary Service.

Displacement	950 to 996 tons normal trim
Measurement	992 tons gross, 269 to 283 tons deadweight
Dimensions	*Goosander* and *Pochard:* $196\frac{3}{4}$ including horns $\times$ $39\frac{1}{3}$ $\times$ $10\frac{1}{4}$ feet
	Garganey and *Goldeneye:* 190 including horns $\times$ $36\frac{1}{2}$ $\times$ $10\frac{3}{4}$ feet
	Mandarin and *Pintail:* 182 including horns $\times$ $36\frac{1}{2}$ $\times$ $10\frac{3}{4}$ feet
Machinery	1 Davey Paxman 16-cylinder diesel, 1 shaft. Controllable pitch propeller. bhp : 600 = 10 knots
Complement	24 naval or 25 civil (*Goosander* and *Pochard* 32)

	No.	Builders	Launched	Completed
Garganey	P 194	Brooke Marine Ltd, Lowestoft	13 Dec. 1965	Sep. 1966
Goldeneye	P 195	Brooke Marine Ltd, Lowestoft	31 Mar. 1966	Jan. 1967
Goosander	P 196	Robb Caledon, Leith	12 Apr. 1973	Sep. 1973
Mandarin	P 192	Cammell, Laird & Co. Ltd, Birkenhead	17 Sep. 1963	Mar. 1964
Pintail	P 193	Cammell, Laird & Co. Ltd, Birkenhead	3 Dec. 1963	June 1964
Pochard	P 197	Robb Caledon, Leith	21 June 1973	Dec. 1973

MANDARIN

LAYBURN   LAYMOOR

This pair of specialized vessels, of which *Laymoor* was the prototype and actually the 'name-ship' of the class, have naturally become known as the 'Lay' class. They were the first boom defence vessels to have been designed and built as such since the end of the Second World War and construction of both was awarded to the same firm to ensure standardization of specifications and uniformity of inspection. In addition to their ability to lay and maintain the latest types of underwater and surface boom defences, first class warship moorings and navigational buoys, they can undertake minor salvage work and the towing of net sections. Their lifting capacity is much greater than that of their predecessors. An improvement in accommodation and general habitability standards enables the ships to be comfortably operated both in the tropics and in cold climates. They were designed for naval or civilian manning, but they are actually shown in the Navy List proper and not under the Royal Maritime Auxiliary Service.

Displacement	800 tons standard, 1 050 tons full load
Dimensions	$192\frac{3}{4} \times 34\frac{1}{2} \times 11\frac{1}{2}$ feet
Machinery	Triple expansion steam reciprocating, 1 shaft, ihp: 1 300 = 10 knots
Boilers	2 Foster Wheeler 'D' Type forced draught
Complement	31 to 36 naval personnel

	No.	Builders	Launched	Completed
Layburn	P 191	Wm. Simons & Co. Ltd (Simons-Lobnitz Ltd)	14 Apr. 1960	7 July 1960
Laymoor	P 190	Wm. Simons & Co. Ltd (Simons-Lobnitz Ltd)	6 Aug. 1959	9 Dec. 1959

LAYBURN *Official*

MOORHEN   MOORLAND   MOORSMAN

These vessels are the survivors of a large group of seventeen units built during 1938 to 1946 which although of varying displacements and dimensions were nevertheless collectively known as the 'Moor' class. They were employed as mooring, salvage and boom vessels from the outset, and were fitted with salvage pumps, air compressors, and diving equipment. *Moorsman* is of the largest type built by HM Dockyard, Chatham, while *Moorland* is of the smallest type built by Goole Shipbuilding & Repair Co. Ltd. *Moorhen* and *Moorland*, eventually for disposal, were allocated as Port Auxiliary Service craft at Malta and Gibraltar respectively. *Moorsman*, at Greenock in the Royal Maritime Auxiliary Service, is also civilian manned. Of the remainder of the 'Moor' group, *Moordale* was sold in 1961, *Moorburn* was declared for disposal in 1962, *Mooress* and *Moorfowl* were placed on the disposal list in 1963, *Moorcock* was broken up at Troon in 1963, *Moorfield* was sold to Pounds Shipowners and Shipbreakers Ltd, Portsmouth, *Moorfire* was broken up on the Forth, *Moorfly* was sold as *Sophia G*, *Moorgrass* was broken up at Troon, *Moorgrieve* was sold and became *Octopus* in 1965, *Moorhill* was sold as Portuguese mercantile, *Moormyrtle* was broken up at Cork and *Moorside* was broken up on the Forth. *Moorpout* was recently listed for disposal.

Displacement	*Moorsman:* 1 040 tons standard, 1 510 tons full load
	Moorhen: 650 tons standard, 900 tons full load
	Moorland: 600 tons standard, 800 tons full load
Dimensions	*Moorsman:* 196 overall × 35½ × 13½ feet
	Moorhen: 196 over horns × 30 × 12 feet
	Moorland: 145 over hull × 30 × 12 feet
Machinery	*Moorsman:* hp : 1 000 = 10 knots
	Moorhen: ihp : 500 = 9 knots
	Moorland: ihp : 500 = 9 knots
Complement	24 to 34

Other civilian manned mooring and salvage vessels listed under the Royal Maritime Auxiliary Service in the Navy List are: *Eminent, LC 10, LC 11, Miner III* (former controlled minelayer, now diving tender) and *Seamoor*.

MOORSMAN

Official

DISPENSER KINBRACE KINGARTH KINLOSS SUCCOUR SWIN UPLIFTER

These ships, generally known as the 'Kin' class, were originally classified as Coastal Salvage Vessels, but they were rerated as Mooring, Salvage and Boom Vessels in 1971. All are equipped with lifting horns and heavy rollers forward, and they can lift 200 tons deadweight over the bows. *Uplifter,* laid down on 13 February 1943 and completed on 6 April 1944, was the only salvage vessel wearing the White Ensign. (*Kingarth* wore the White Ensign in 1957.) *Dispenser,* launched on 22 April 1943, was on charter to Liverpool & Glasgow Salvage Association, but returned in 1971 and is shown as a mooring and salvage vessel under the Royal Maritime Auxiliary Service in the Navy List. *Succour* and *Swin* were Royal Fleet Auxiliaries wearing the Blue Ensign, but *Succour* was listed under the Royal Maritime Auxiliary Service recently, as was *Kinloss,* formerly in the Port Auxiliary Service. The latter was refitted with diesel engines in 1963–64 and *Kinbrace, Kingarth* and *Uplifter* were similarly re-engined in 1966–67.

Displacement	950 tons standard, 1 050 tons full load
Measurement	775 tons gross, 262 tons deadweight
Dimensions	$179\frac{1}{2} \times 35\frac{1}{4} \times 12$ feet
Machinery	*Kinbrace, Kingarth, Kinloss, Uplifter:*
	1 British Polar Atlas diesel, bhp : 630 = 9 knots
	Others:
	Triple expansion steam reciprocating, 1 shaft,
	ihp : 600 = 9 knots
Boilers	*Others:*
	1 return tube cylindrical
Complement	34

	No.	Builders	Launched
Kinbrace	A 281	Alexander Hall & Co. Ltd, Aberdeen	17 Jan. 1945
Kingarth	A 232	Alexander Hall & Co. Ltd, Aberdeen	22 May 1944
Kinloss	A 482	Alexander Hall & Co. Ltd, Aberdeen	14 Apr. 1945
Succour	A 505	Smith's Dock Co. Ltd, South Bank-on-Tees	18 Aug. 1943
Swin	A 506	Alexander Hall & Co. Ltd, Aberdeen	25 Mar. 1944
Uplifter	A 507	Smith's Dock Co. Ltd, South Bank-on-Tees	29 Nov. 1943

KINBRACE

BARBAIN   BARFOOT   BARFOIL   BARMOND

These are the only surviving representatives of the numerically very large class of combined boom defence vessels and netlayers built just before and during the Second World War which ran into a total of 71 ships, although four others are still shown in the Navy List, namely *Barnard*, *Barnstone* (in reserve), *Barrage* and *Barrington* (in reserve), at the time of writing. They were designed for a bow lift of 27 to 70 tons. *Barhill* and *Barndale* were allocated as Port Auxiliary Service (PAS) craft, and *Barfoot* and *Barmond* are also civilian manned in the Royal Maritime Auxiliary Service. *Barfoil* is in commission with a naval ship's company, according to the latest Navy List, but the status of *Barbain* is not given. Ships of the class transferred were *Barbrake* and *Barcross* to South Africa, *Barbarian*, *Barbette* (first of this name in the class, launched on 15 December 1937) and *Barfair* to Turkey, and *Baron* to Ceylon in 1958 (purchased by the Colombo Port Commission). Of the remainder of the class *Barflake* and *Barlight* were lost during the Second World War and *Barbour*, *Bardell* and *Barricade* were discarded, *Barberry*, *Barbrook*, *Barcombe*, *Barford*, *Baritone*, *Barlane*, *Barlow*, *Barmill*, *Barneath* and *Barnwell* were declared for disposal in 1958, *Barilla* and *Baronia* in 1959, *Bartholm* and *Barstoke* in 1960, *Barbette* (second of the class with this name, accepted into service on 12 July 1943), *Barbridge*, *Barcastle*, *Barcock*, *Barcote*, *Barcroft*, *Bardolf*, *Barlake*, *Barsing*, *Barsound*, *Barthorpe* and *Barrier* in 1962, *Barbourne*, *Barclose*, *Barking*, *Barspear* and *Barwind* in 1963, *Barbastel*, *Barfount*, *Barkis*, *Barleycorn*, *Barmouth*, *Barnaby*, *Barnehurst*, *Barova*, *Barranca* and *Barrhead* in 1964, *Bartisan* in 1966, *Barcarole*, *Barcliffe*, *Barbican*, *Barfoam* and *Barfoss* in 1969, *Barbecue*, *Barfield*, *Barglow*, *Barhill* and *Barndale* in 1971.

Displacement	750 tons standard, 1 000 tons full load
Dimensions	182 over horns $\times$ 23$\frac{1}{4}$ $\times$ 11$\frac{1}{2}$ feet
Machinery	Triple expansion, ihp: 850 = 11 knots, 9 knots sea speed
Boilers	2 single ended (oil fired in *Barmond*)
Complement	32

	No.	Builders	Launched
Barbain	P 201	Blyth Drydocks and Shipbuilding Company	8 Jan. 1940
Barfoot	P 202	John Lewis & Sons Ltd, Aberdeen	25 Sep. 1942
Barfoil	P 294	Philip & Son Ltd, Dartmouth	18 July 1942
Barmond	P 232	Wm Simons & Co. Ltd, Renfrew	24 Dec. 1942

BARFOOT

SALVALOUR   SALVEDA   SEA SALVOR

Two of these ocean salvage vessels are in the Navy List proper, in reserve, namely *Salvalour* and *Salveda,* while the third, *Sea Salvor,* was in a recent Navy List under the Royal Fleet Auxiliary Service with an active status. *Salveda* was formerly a Royal Fleet Auxiliary ocean salvage vessel on charter to Metal Industries Ltd. All the ships of the 'Salv' class were of practically uniform design except *Salveda* which is considerably larger, see data below. Of sister ships transferred, *Salventure* was loaned to the Royal Hellenic Navy and renamed *Sotir; King Salvor* was converted into a submarine rescue bell ship for the Royal Navy in 1953–54 and renamed *Kingfisher,* but was sold to Argentina in December 1960, sailing to Argentina in April 1961 under the new naval name *Tehuelche* and again renamed *Guardiamarina Zicari* by the Argentine Navy in 1963. Of the remaining ships of the class, *Salvage Duke,* formerly on charter to the Turkish Salvage Administration and renamed *Imroz,* was gutted by fire in 1959; *Ocean Salvor* and *Salviola* were disposed of in 1960, and *Prince Salvor* and *Salvigil* were sold in 1968. *Salvestor* and *Salvictor* were sold in July 1970 to Ward (Briton Ferry) but they were shown in the 1972 Navy List as in reserve.

Salveda:	Displacement	1 440 tons standard, 1 700 tons full load
	Measurement	1 122 tons gross
	Dimensions	$216 \times 37\frac{3}{4} \times 13$ feet
	Machinery	Triple expansion, 2 shafts, ihp : 1 500 = 12 knots
	Complement	72
Salvalour		
Sea Salvor:	Displacement	1 250 tons standard, 1 360 tons full load
	Dimensions	$194 \times 34\frac{1}{2} \times 11\frac{1}{4}$ feet
	Machinery	hp : 1 200 = 12 knots
	Complement	62

	No.	*Builders*	*Launched*
Salvalour	A 494	Goole Shipbuilding & Repair Co. Ltd	2 Nov. 1944
Salveda	A 497	Cammell, Laird & Co. Ltd	9 Feb. 1943
Sea Salvor:	A 503	Goole Shipbuilding & Repair Co. Ltd	22 Apr. 1943

SEA SALVOR *Lennon*

BULLFINCH

ST MARGARETS

These two specialized vessels are under the jurisdiction of the Royal Maritime Auxiliary Service with superintendence from the RMAS base at Turnchapel, Plymouth. They each have an officer complement of eleven. In their construction provision was made for mounting one four-inch-calibre gun and four 20-mm anti-aircraft guns, but no armament is actually fitted. Two sister ships, *Bullfrog* and *Bullhead*, of this type were transferred to the Cable and Wireless service in 1947, but the remaining two ships are still known as the 'Bull' class.

Displacement	1 300 tons light, 2 500 tons full load
Measurement	1 524 tons gross, 1 200 tons deadweight
Dimensions	$252 \times 36\frac{1}{2} \times 16\frac{1}{3}$ feet
Machinery	Triple expansion steam reciprocating engines, 2 shafts, ihp: 1 250 = 12 knots
Complement	71
Builders	Swan, Hunter & Wigham Richardson Ltd, Wallsend-on-Tyne
Launched	*Bullfinch:* 19 August 1940
	St Margarets: 13 October 1943
Pennant nos.	*Bullfinch:* A 176
	St Margarets: A 259

MFV Types (see under Fleet Tenders on page 162):

MFV 1527, MFV 1544. Two in Port Auxiliary Service. Length 90 feet.

MFV 1021, 1033, 1037, 1048, 1051, 1062, 1077, 1079, 1151, 1164 1190, 1206, 1215, 1219, 1255, 1256, 1257. Eighteen in Port Auxiliary Service. Length 75 feet.

MFV 2, 9, 15, 57, 63, 74, 84, 88, 93, 96, 97, 119, 123, 133, 136, 139, 140, 158, 175, 205, 238, 256, 278, 289, 323. Twenty-five in Port Auxiliary Service. Length 61½ feet.

MFV 642, 658, 686, 637, 715, 737, 740, 742, 767, 773, 775, 815, 816, 867, 911, 944. Sixteen in Port Auxiliary Service. Length 45 feet.

Two named *Squirrel*, MFV 1151, and *Watchful*, MFV 1080, were used as Fishery Protection Gunboats until replaced. MFVs 105, 1021 and 1528 were deleted from the Navy List in 1969, MFVs 7, 43, 45, 64, 65, 627, 657, 673 and 1254 in 1970, and 1015 in 1971.

BULLFINCH *Official*

Landing Ships: **EMPIRE GULL** (ex-*Trouncer* LST (3) 3513) is in the Navy List under the Royal Fleet Auxiliary Service. Displacement 2 140 tons light, 5 000 tons full load; dimensions $347\frac{1}{2} \times 55\frac{1}{4} \times 12$ feet; machinery triple expansion, 2 shafts, 5 500 ihp = 13 knots, boilers 2 Admiralty 3-drum type. Of the many tank landing ships of the LST(A), LST(3) and LST(Q) types most have now been disposed of, but *Anzio* (ex-LST(A) 3003), *Dieppe* (ex-LST(3) 3016), harbour accommodation ship, *Messina* (ex-LST(C) 3043), *Narvik* (ex-LST(C) 3044), accommodation ship, *Stalker* (ex-LST(3) 3515), *Striker* (ex-LST (A) 3516), *Tracker* (ex-LST(3) 3522) and *Zeebrugge* (ex-LST(3) 3532) were still in the most recently published Navy List. *Landing Craft:* LCM(9) 700 to LCM(9) 711, LCM(9) 3507 and LCM(9) 3508. Most of these 14 craft, 75 tons light, 176 tons loaded, are allocated to assault ships. There are also 10 MRC (ex-LCT) maintenance and repair craft, former tank landing craft, 2 LCM(7), 29 LCVP and 2 LCP(L)3.
(**AACHEN** L 4062, **ABBEVILLE** L 4041, **AGHEILA** L 4002, **AKYAB** (ex-*Rampart*) L 4037, **ANDALNES** L 4097, **ANTWERP** L 4074, **AREZZO** L 4128, **ARAKAN** L 4164 and **AUDEMER** L 4061 are landing craft of the LCT(8) type, 657 tons light, 1 017 tons loaded, $231\frac{1}{4} \times 39 \times 5$ feet, 4 Paxman diesels, 1 840 bhp, speed $12\frac{2}{3}$ knots, complement 37, transferred from the Royal Navy to the Army.)
Controlled Minelayers: **MINER III** (N 13) is the only controlled minelayer of a class of 8 known as the 'Miner' class remaining in the Navy List and is in the Royal Maritime Auxiliary Service as a diving tender at Pembroke dock: 300 tons standard, 355 tons full load, $110\frac{1}{4} \times 26\frac{1}{2} \times 8$ feet, Ruston & Hornsby diesels, 2 shafts, 360 bhp = 10 knots. Of her two surviving sisters **BRITANNIC** (ex-*Miner V,* N 15) was converted into a cable lighter and renamed in 1960 and is with the Port Auxiliary Service as store carrier, and **STEADY** was adapted as a stabilization trials ship at Portsmouth and renamed in 1960 with the PAS.
Torpedo Recovery Vessels: **TORRENT** A 127 and **TORRID** A 128 are new specialized vessels custom built for the job instead of vessels converted from other categories as formerly. Displacement 550 tons full load, measurement 405 tons gross, length 151 feet, Paxman diesels, 700 bhp = 12 knots. Built as TRVs, both by Clelands, launched on 29 Mar. 1971 and 7 Sep. 1971 respectively, and completed in Sep. 1971 and Jan. 1972.
Tank Cleaning Vessels (Minesweeping Trawlers): The following eight ships of the 'Isles' class, named with builders and launch dates, are former minesweeping trawlers converted to tank cleaning vessels. **COLL** A 333, **GRAEMSAY** A 340, Ardrossan Dockyard Co. Ltd, 7 Apr. 1942, 3 Aug. 1942; **BERN, LUNDY,** A 334, A 336, Cook Welton & Gemmell Ltd, Beverley, 2 May 1942, 29 Aug. 1942; **SWITHA** A 346, 3 Apr. 1942, A. & J. Inglis Ltd, Glasgow; **CALDY** A 332, 31 Aug. 1943, **FOULNESS** A 342, 23 May 1943, **SKOMER** A 338, 17 June 1943, John Lewis & Sons Ltd, Aberdeen. 560 tons standard, 770 tons full load, $164 \times 27\frac{1}{2} \times 14$ feet, triple expansion engines, 1 shaft, 850 bhp = 12 knots, 1 cylindrical boiler, coal 183 tons. Classed as Port Auxiliary Service vessels with 300 series pennant numbers. Sister ship *Bardsey,* also converted, was taken over by Malta Dockyard.

TORRENT

Official

Nuclear Decontamination Vessel: **MAC** 1012. This unusual vessel was specifically built as a nuclear decontamination vessel in HM Dockyard, Chatham, and was designed to be used in connection with the disposal of radioactive waste from pipes in nuclear powered submarines at the Medway naval base refitting complex for reactor plants in those highly sophisticated naval vessels. Launched on 10 Feb. 1971, she has a length of 185 feet and a beam of 35 feet.

Armament Carriers: **KINTERBURY** A 378, **THROSK**, both built by Philip & Son Ltd, Dartmouth, and launched on 14 Nov. 1942 and in 1943 and completed on 4 Mar. 1943 and 22 Dec. 1943 respectively. Rated as naval armament carriers. Converted in 1959 with hold stowage and a derrick for handling guided missiles for attending and servicing the guided missiles trials ship *Girdle Ness*. *Kinterbury* is in the Port Auxiliary Service. Displacement 1 490 tons standard, 1 770 tons full load, measurement 600 tons deadweight, dimensions $200 \times 34\frac{1}{3} \times 13$ feet, triple expansion engines, 1 shaft, 900 ihp = 11 knots, coal, 154 tons.

MAXIM A 377, **NORDENFELT** A 135, built by Lobnitz & Co. Ltd, Renfrew, launched on 6 Aug. 1945 and 30 Nov. 1945, respectively. Displacement 663 tons, measurement 340 tons deadweight, $144\frac{1}{2} \times 25 \times 8$ feet, reciprocating engines, 500 ihp = 9 knots, complement 13. Of sisters, *Chattenden* was reduced to a dumb derrick lighter in 1961, *Snider, Enfield* and *Gatling* were disposed of in 1968–70. *Nordenfelt* is in reserve.

BALLISTA, BOWSTRING, CATAPULT, FLINTLOCK, MATCHLOCK, SPEAR. All in the Port Auxiliary Service. Of various displacements and data. Sister ships *Blowpipe* and *Obus* were sold. *Spear* is in reserve.

Store Carriers: **ROBERT MIDDLETON** A 241, built by Grangemouth Dockyard Co. Ltd, launched on 29 June 1938, displacement 900 tons light, 1 900 tons full load, measurement 1 000 tons deadweight, 1 125 tons gross, dimensions 220 $\times 35 \times 13\frac{1}{2}$, Atlas Polar diesel, 1 shaft, 960 bhp = $10\frac{1}{2}$ knots, complement 17. In the Royal Fleet Auxiliary Service. Sister ship *Robert Dundas* was sold in 1972.

THOMAS GRANT, built as a local store carrier by Charles Hill & Sons Ltd, Bristol, launched on 11 May and completed in July 1953. Turned over to the Port Auxiliary Service in 1959 under Dockyard administration at Portsmouth. Converted into a torpedo recovery vessel in 1968. Displacement 209 tons light, 461 tons full load, measurement 252 tons deadweight, 218 tons gross, $113\frac{1}{2} \times 25\frac{1}{2} \times 8\frac{3}{4}$ feet, 2 Mirrlees 5-cyl. diesels, 2 shafts, 500 bhp = 10 knots.

Water Carriers: 'Water' class, **WATERFALL** Y 17, **WATERSHED** Y 18, **WATERSIDE** Y 20, **WATERSPOUT** Y 19, built by Drypool Engineering & Drydock Co., Hull, launched on 30 Mar. 1966, 3 Aug. 1966, 20 June 1967 and 29 Dec. 1966 respectively, measurement 285 tons gross, $131\frac{1}{2} \times 24\frac{3}{4} \times 8$ feet, diesels, 1 shaft, 1 100 bhp = 11 knots.

'Spa' class, **SPALAKE** A 260, **SPAPOOL** A 222, **SPABROOK** A 224, **SPABURN** A 257, displacement 1 219 tons full load, measurement 630 tons deadweight, 719 tons gross, $172 \times 30 \times 12$ feet, triple expansion engines, 675 ihp = 9 knots, 90 tons coal. Originally carried one 3-inch gun and two 20-mm anti-aircraft guns. Built by Charles Hill & Sons Ltd, Bristol (first two), and Philip & Son Ltd, Dartmouth, launched on 10 Aug. 1946, 28 Feb. 1946, 24 Aug. 1944, 5 Jan. 1946 respectively; *Spapool* is with the Port Auxiliary Service; *Spabeck*, high test peroxide carrier for the experimental submarine *Explorer*, was disposed of in May 1966 and *Spa* in 1970.

KINTERBURY

'Fresh' class, **FRESHBURN, FRESHLAKE, FRESHMERE, FRESHPOND, FRESHPOOL, FRESHSPRING,** all built in 1940 to 1946 and originally armed with two 20-mm anti-aircraft guns, displacement 594 tons, dimensions $126\frac{1}{4} \times 25\frac{1}{2} \times 10\frac{3}{4}$ feet, triple expansion steam reciprocating engines, 450 ihp = 8 knots. *Freshspring* was converted from coal burning to oil fuel firing in 1961. *Freshpool* is in reserve. Of sister ships, *Freshbrook* and *Freshnet* were discarded in 1963, *Freshwater* and *Freshwell* were sold in 1968 and *Freshford, Freshspray* and *Freshtarn* in 1969. *Freshener* was for disposal in 1971.

Fleet Tenders: 'Insect' class, **BEE** 5 June 1969, **CICALA** 22 June 1970, **CRICKET** 30 Aug. 1969, **GNAT** 25 Nov. 1969, **LADYBIRD** 27 Jan. 1970, **SCARAB,** displacement 450 tons full load, 200 tons deadweight measurement, dimensions $111\frac{3}{4} \times 28 \times 11$ feet, machinery Lister Blackstone Lister 8-cyl. diesel. 1 shaft, 660 bhp = $10\frac{1}{2}$ knots, complement 10. All built by C. D. Holmes Ltd, Beverley, Yorks, see launch dates above after names. These vessels are of a much improved design as compared with the modified fleet tenders of the interim 'Cartmel' class, enlarged all round to undertake coastal voyages. All six have practically identical hull particulars and propelling machinery, but the first three built, *Bee, Cricket* and *Gnat,* were fitted out as store carriers and rigged with two cranes, and the next pair, *Ladybird* and *Cicala,* were adapted as armament store carriers and equipped with a two-ton crane, while *Scarab* emerged in Nov. 1971 as a mooring vessel with a three-ton crane and rigged to lift ten tons over the bow.

'Cartmel' class, **CARTMEL, CAWSAND, CLOVELLY, CRICCIETH,** Pimblott & Sons, Northwich, **CRICKLADE,** C. D. Holmes Ltd, **CROMARTY,** J. Lewis, Aberdeen, **DENMEAD,** C. D. Holmes, **DORNOCH,** J. Lewis, **DUNSTER,** R. Dunston, Thorne, **ELKSTONE, ELSING, EPWORTH, ETTRICK,** J. Cook, Wivenhoe, **FELSTED,** R. Dunston, **FINTRY,** J. Lewis, **FOTHERBY, FROXFIELD,** R. Dunston, **FULBECK,** C. D. Holmes, **GLENCOVE,** Pimblott, **GRASMERE,** J. Lewis, **LOYAL FACTOR** (A 382), C. D. Holmes, **LOYAL GOVERNOR** (A 510), Pimblott. These general purpose craft are of a modified design as compared with the original fleet tenders of the 'Aberdovey' class. (See builders after names above.) All are of round bilge hull form. Displacement 143 tons full load, measurement 25 tons deadweight, dimensions $80 \times 21 \times 6\frac{1}{2}$ feet, machinery 1 Lister Blackstone 4-cyl. diesel, 1 shaft, 320 bhp = $10\frac{1}{2}$ knots, complement 6. Ten are fitted as store carriers only, ten as store and passenger carriers, and the last pair as Royal Fleet Auxiliary Service training transports (fitted to accommodate 12 personnel). Eight further units being completed were ordered from R. Dunston.

DATCHET. Diving tender launched by Vosper Thornycroft, Portsmouth, on 18 Feb. 1968. Steel hull with wooden superstructure. Fitted with a compression chamber on deck, handled by a derrick. Displacement 70 tons, $75 \times 19 \times 4$ feet, Gray diesels, 2 shafts, 450 bhp = 12 knots, crew 5.

'Aberdovey' class, all built in 1963–65 : **ABERDOVEY, ABINGER, ALNESS, ALNMOUTH, APPLEBY, ASHCOTT,** built by Isaac Pimblott & Sons, Northwich, **BEAULIEU, BEDDGELERT, BEMBRIDGE, BIBURY, BLAKENEY, BRODICK** (J. S. Doig Ltd, Grimsby). The first post-war fleet tenders. Displacement $117\frac{1}{2}$ tons full load, measurement 70 tons gross, 25 tons deadweight, dimensions $79\frac{3}{4} \times 18 \times 5\frac{1}{2}$ feet, 1 Lister Blackstone diesel, 1 shaft, 225 bhp = $10\frac{1}{2}$ knots, crew 6. Built to Lloyd's Register requirements and constructed from 12 prefabricated sections. Designed to carry up to 3 000 cu. ft of stores or 200 standing passengers in addition to two 21-inch torpedoes each of 1.8 tons.

SPALAKE

Pavia

ROBUST   ROLLICKER   ROYSTERER

The *Roysterer*, prototype of this new 'Ro' class, was the largest and most powerful oceangoing tug built for the Royal Navy for many years. She was designed primarily for salvage and long range towage but she can be used for general harbour duties. These vessels are now part of the Royal Maritime Auxiliary Service.

Displacement	1 630 tons full load
Dimensions	178 × 38½ × 21⅓ feet
Machinery	2 Mirrlees diesels, 2 shafts, bhp : 4 500 = 15 knots
Complement	31 (and able to carry naval salvage party of 10)
Builders	Charles D. Holmes, Beverley Shipyard, Hull
Launched	20 Apr. 1970 (*Roysterer*), 29 Jan. 1971 (*Rollicker*) and 7 Oct. 1971

TYPHOON

Completed in 1960 with diesels manufactured by Vickers-Armstrongs Ltd, Barrow. The machinery arrangement of two diesels geared to a single shaft was an innovation for naval oceangoing tugs. This 'one-off' vessel is fitted for fire fighting, salvage and ocean rescue, with a heavy mainmast and derrick attached. Formerly a Royal Fleet Auxiliary, she is now in the Royal Maritime Auxiliary Service. Pennant no. A 95.

Displacement	800 tons standard, 1 380 tons full load
Dimensions	200 × 40 × 13 feet
Machinery	2 turbocharged V type 12-cyl. diesels, bhp : 2 750 = 16 knots
Complement	33
Builders	Henry Robb & Co. Ltd, Leith
Launched	14 Oct. 1958

ACCORD   ADEPT   ADVICE   AGILE   CONFIANCE   CONFIDENT

Accord, Advice and *Agile,* formerly rated as dockyard tugs, as *Adept* still is, were officially added to the 'Con' class in 1971 as part of the Royal Maritime Auxiliary Service ocean towing force. Fitted with Stone Kamewa controllable pitch propellers. All built by A & J Inglis Ltd, Glasgow, except *Agile* by Goole Shipbuilding & Repair Co. Ltd.

Displacement	760 tons full load
Dimensions	155½ ('Con' pair 154¾) × 35 × 13 feet ('Con' 11)
Guns	One 40-mm anti-aircraft
Machinery	4 Davey Paxman 12-cyl. diesels, 2 shafts, bhp : 1 600 = 13 knots
Complement	29 plus 13 salvage party
Launched	*Accord* A 90, 17 Sep. 1957 ; *Advice* A 89, 16 Oct. 1958 ; *Agile* A 88, 2 July 1957 ; *Confiance,* A 289 15 Nov. 1955 ; *Confident* A 290, 17 Jan. 1956

ROYSTERER *Official*

SAMSON   SEA GIANT   SUPERMAN

All these large tugs of oceangoing dimensions were built and engined by Alexander Hall & Co Ltd, Aberdeen, and launched on 14 May 1953, 2 June 1954 and 23 November 1953 respectively. They are generally referred to as the 'Samson' class or 'Giant' class.

Displacement	900 tons standard, 1 200 tons full load
Measurement	850 tons gross
Dimensions	180 × 37 × 14 feet
Machinery	Triple expansion steam reciprocating engines, 2 shafts, ihp: 3 000 = 15 to 16 knots
Complement	30 average
Pennant nos.	A 390 (*Samson*), A 288 (*Sea Giant*)

CAPABLE   CAREFUL   NIMBLE

These vessels, which measure up to oceangoing duties, originally constituted a class of four officially designated the 'Nimble' class but sometimes known as the 'Capable' class. *Capable* was fitted experimentally with controllable pitch propellers. The fourth ship of the type, *Expert,* was disposed of in October 1968. Rated as fleet tugs. Armament removed.

Displacement	890 tons standard, 1 190 tons full load
Dimensions	175 × $35\frac{3}{4}$ × $13\frac{3}{4}$ feet
Machinery	Triple expansion steam reciprocating engines, 2 shafts, ihp: 3 500 = 16 knots
Boilers	2 of three-drum type
Complement	33

	No.	Builders	Launched
Capable	A 508	Hall, Russell & Co. Ltd, Aberdeen	22 Nov. 1945
Careful	A 293	Alexander Hall & Co. Ltd, Aberdeen	23 Oct. 1945
Nimble	A 223	Fleming & Ferguson Ltd, Paisley	4 Dec. 1941

Of the tugs of the 'Envoy' class, *Enticer* was lost on 21 Dec. 1946, *Enforcer* and *Enigma* were stricken from the list in 1963, *Envoy* was sold in 1965 as *Matsas,* and *Encore* was sold in 1968 as *Salvaliant.*

SAMSON   *Official*

BUSTLER   CYCLONE (*ex-Growler*)   SAMSONIA   REWARD

All these largest oceangoing tugs were formerly in the Royal Fleet Auxiliary Service, but are now listed under the Royal Maritime Auxiliary Service in the Navy List. They were all built by Henry Robb Ltd, Leith. *Growler,* temporarily renamed *Caroline Moller* while on long term charter, then renamed *Castle Peak,* was returned to the Royal Fleet Auxiliary Service in 1957, then renamed *Welshman* and chartered to the United Towing Co. Ltd, and again renamed *Cyclone* on return to the RFAS in 1964. Most of this class, including *Reward* to United Towing Co. Ltd in 1963, and *Turmoil* to Overseas Towage & Salvage Co., were chartered by commercial undertakings. *Bustler* latterly wore the Blue Ensign. Of this class *Hesperia* was lost during the Second World War; HMS *Mediator,* the last tug to sail under the White Ensign and not the Blue Ensign of the RFAS, was paid off in 1964 and sold in 1968 as *Nisos Zakynthos*; *Turmoil* was sold in 1965 as *Nisos Kerkyra*; and *Warden* was disposed of in November 1969.

Displacement	1 118 tons light, 1 630 tons full load
Dimensions	205 × 40¼ × 16¾ feet
Machinery	2 Atlas Polar 8-cylinder diesels, 1 shaft, bhp : 4 000 = 16 knots
Guns	One 3-inch and one 40-mm anti-aircraft originally (removed)
Complement	42

	No.	Launched		No.	Launched
Bustler	A 240	4 Dec. 1941	*Samsonia*	A 218	1 Apr. 1942
Cyclone	A 111	10 Sep. 1942	*Reward*	A 264	13 Oct. 1944

Small fleet servicing and coastal harbour tugs include *Empire Ace* (ex-*Diligent*), *Empire Demon, Empire Fred, Empire Ross, Frisky* (ex-*Empire Rita*) and *Resolve* (ex-*Empire Zona*), but not all are of the same type.
Tugs in the Port Auxiliary Service include *Bombshell, Cannon, Chainshot, Diver, Driver, Eminent, Fidget, Foremost, Freedom, Grapeshot, Handmaid, Impetus, Integrity, Prompt, Resolve, Security, Tampion, Trunnion, Vagrant* and *Weasel.* Also the water tractor *Felicity,* a small improved 'Girl' class berthing tug for basin work built by Richard Dunstan Ltd, Hull.

SAMSONIA

DEXTEROUS
DIRECTOR

FAITHFUL
FAVOURITE
FORCEFUL

GRINDER
GRIPER

These diesel-electric paddle tugs of seagoing dimensions are employed on roadstead, port approach and harbour service and in the naval bases. Known unofficially as dockyard paddlers but officially designated the 'Director' class, they have raked-back bow, hinged foremast and low funnel, with side paddle propulsion with diesel-electric chain drive for dockyard handling of larger warships. Rated as dockyard tugs.

Displacement	710 tons full load
Dimensions	$157\frac{1}{4} \times 30$ (60 across paddle wheel boxes) × 10 feet
Machinery	4 Davey Paxman 12-cyl. diesels and BTH electric motors, 2 shafts, bhp: 2 000, shp: 1 600 = 13 knots
Complement	21

	No.	Builders	Launched
Dexterous	A 93	Yarrow Ltd, Glasgow	21 Aug. 1956
Director	A 94	Yarrow Ltd, Glasgow	11 June 1956
Faithful	A 85	Yarrow Ltd, Glasgow	14 June 1957
Favourite	A 87	Ferguson Bros, Glasgow	1 July 1958
Forceful	A 86	Yarrow Ltd, Glasgow	20 May 1957
Grinder	A 92	Wm Simons, Renfrew	6 May 1958
Grouper	A 91	Wm Simons, Renfrew	6 Mar. 1958

Other dockyard tugs include the medium berthing tugs *Airedale, Alsatian, Basset, Beagle, Boxer, Cairn, Collie, Corgi, Dalmatian, Deerhound, Elkhound, Husky, Labrador, Mastiff, Pointer, Saluki, Sealyham, Setter, Sheepdog, Spaniel* ('Dog' class) and harbour berthing tugs *Agatha, Agnes, Alice, Audrey, Barbara, Betty, Brenda, Bridget* ('Girl' class), *Celia, Charlotte, Christine, Clare, Daisy, Daphne, Doris, Dorothy, Edith* (Improved 'Girl' class).

FORCEFUL

PICTURE GALLERY SUPPLEMENT

HARRIER over ARK ROYAL

Official

PHANTOM

Official

BUCCANEER *Official*

SEA VIXEN II

Official

GANNETS Mk III

Official

SEA KINGS

Official

LYNX

WHIRLWIND 9

WESSEX 5

Official

WESSEX 3

WESSEX Mk I

Official

WASP

Official

GAZELLE

Westland

SIOUX

Official

POLARIS   *Official*

EXOCET

SEASLUG *Official*

SEA DART *Official*

SEACAT

IKARA

BH 7

SRN 6   *Official*

AIRCRAFT CARRIERS

R 05 Eagle
(R 06 Centaur)
R 07 Albion
R 08 Bulwark
R 09 Ark Royal
R 12 Hermes
(R 38 Victorious)

SUBMARINES

S 01 Porpoise
S 02 Rorqual
S 03 Narwhal
S 04 Grampus
S 05 Finwhale
S 06 Cachalot
S 07 Sealion
S 08 Walrus
S 09 Oberon
S 10 Odin
S 11 Orpheus
S 12 Olympus
S 13 Osiris
S 14 Onslaught
S 15 Otter
S 16 Oracle
S 17 Ocelot
S 18 Otus
S 19 Opossum
S 20 Opportune
S 21 Onyx
S 22 Resolution
S 23 Repulse
S 26 Renown

Submarines—contd.

S 27 Revenge
(S 28 Token)
S 32 Tiptoe
(S 33 Trump)
(S 34 Taciturn)
(S 37 Talent)
(S 41 Alaric)
S 42 Tabard
(S 43 Amphion)
(S 46 Churchill
(S 47 Astute)
S 49 Artemis
S 50 Courageous
(S 55 Thermopylae)
(S 61 Acheron)
S 63 Andrew
(S 64 Anchorite)
S 65 Alcide
(S 66 Alderney)
S 67 Alliance
(S 68 Ambush)
S 69 Auriga
S 72 Aeneas
(S 96 Artful)
S 101 Dreadnought
S 102 Valiant
S 103 Warspite
S 105 Conqueror
S 108 Sovereign
S 109 Superb
S 110 Sceptre
S 126 Swiftsure

CRUISERS

C 20 Tiger
C 34 Lion
C 35 Belfast
C 99 Blake

HELICOPTER SUPPORT SHIPS

(K 07 Lofoten)
K 08 Engadine

DESTROYERS

D 01 Caprice
D 02 Devonshire
(D 05 Daring)
D 06 Hampshire
(D 07 Caesar)
(D 09 Dunkirk)
(D 10 Cassandra)
D 12 Kent
(D 15 Cavendish)
D 16 London
D 18 Antrim
D 19 Glamorgan
D 20 Fife
D 21 Norfolk
(D 22 Aisne)
D 23 Bristol
D 25 Carysfort
(D 31 Broadsword)
(D 32 Camperdown)
D 35 Diamond
D 43 Matapan
(D 44 Lagos)

Destroyers—contd.

D 51 Chevron
(D 61 Chequers)
(D 64 Scorpion)
D 68 Barrosa
(D 70 Solebay)
D 73 Cavalier
(D 77 Trafalgar)
D 80 Sheffield
D 84 Saintes
(D 85 Cambrian)
D 86 Birmingham
(D 86 Agincourt)
D 96 Crossbow
D 97 Corunna
D 108 Cardiff
(D 108 Dainty)
(D 114 Defender)
D 118 Coventry
(D 119 Delight)
D 154 Duchess

FRIGATES

(F 08 Urania)
(F 09 Troubridge)
F 10 Aurora
F 12 Achilles
F 14 Leopard
F 15 Euryalus
F 16 Diomede
F 18 Galatea
(F 19 Terpsichore)
F 27 Lynx

Frigates—contd.

F   28 Cleopatra
(F 29 Verulam)
F   32 Salisbury
F   34 Puma
F   36 Whitby
F   37 Jaguar
F   38 Arethusa
F   39 Naiad
F   40 Sirius
(F 41 Volage)
F   42 Phoebe
F   43 Torquay
(F 44 Tenacious)
F   45 Minerva
F   47 Danae
F   48 Dundas
(F 50 Venus)
(F 51 ·Grafton)
F   52 Juno
F   53 Undaunted
F· 54 Hardy
F   56 Argonaut
F   57 Andromeda
F   58 Hermione
F   59 Chichester
F   60 Jupiter
F   61 Llandaff
(F 62 Pellew)
F   63 Scarborough
F   65 Tenby
(F 67 Tyrian)
F   69 Bacchante
F   70 Apollo
F   71 Scylla
F   72 Ariadne
(F 72 Wizard)
F   73 Eastbourne

Frigates—contd.

F   75 Charybdis
(F 76 Virago)
F   77 Blackpool
F   78 Blackwood
F   80 Duncan
F   83 Ulster
F   84 Exmouth
F   85 Keppel
F   88 Malcolm
(F 91 Murray)
F   94 Palliser
F   97 Russell
F   99 Lincoln
F 101 Yarmouth
(F 102 Zest)
F 103 Lowestoft
F 104 Dido
F 106 Brighton
F 107 Rothesay
F 108 Londonderry
F 109 Leander
F 113 Falmouth
F 114 Ajax
F 115 Berwick
F 117 Ashanti
F 119 Eskimo
(F 121 Tumult)
F 122 Gurkha
F 124 Zulu
F 125 Mohawk
F 126 Plymouth
F 127 Penelope
F 129 Rhyl
F 131 Nubian
F 133 Tartar
F 138 Rapid
(F 156 Tuscan)

Frigates—contd.

(F 159 Wakeful)
F 169 Amazon
F 170 Antelope
F 171 Active
F 172 Ambuscade
F 173 Arrow
F 174 Ardent
F 175 Alacrity
F 176 Avenger
(F 185 Relentless)
(F 187 Whirlwind)
(F 189 Termagant)
(F 193 Rocket)
(F 196 Urchin)
F 197 Grenville
(F 200 Ursa)
(F 390 Loch Fada)
(F 429 Loch Fyne)
(F 628 Loch Killisport)

MINELAYERS

(N 11 Minstrel (Miner I))
(N 12 Gossamer (Miner II))
N 13 Miner III
(N 14 Miner IV)
(N 15 Britannic (Miner V))
(N 16 Miner VI)
(N 17 Steady (Miner VII))
N 21 Abdiel
(N 26 Plover)
(N 70 Manxman)

LANDING SHIPS

L   10 Fearless (ex-L 3004)
L   11 Intrepid (ex-L 3005)
L 3004 Sir Bedivere
L 3005 Sir Galahad

Landing Ships—contd.

(L 3016 Dieppe)
L 3029 Sir Lancelot
L 3036 Sir Percival
L 3037 Sir Geraint
(L 3043 Messina)
(L 3044 Narvik)
L 3505 Sir Tristram
L 3513 Empire Gull
          (Trouncer L 3523)
(L 3515 Stalker)
(L 3516 Striker)
(L 3522 Tracker)
(L 3532 Zeebrugge)
(L 4038 Citadel)
(L 4044 Portcullis)

AUXILIARIES/ SUPPORT SHIPS

A   00 Britannia
A   70 Echo
A   71 Enterprise
A   72 Egeria
A   75 Tidespring
A   76 Tidepool
A   77 Pearleaf
A   78 Plumleaf
A   79 Bayleaf
A   80 Orangeleaf
A   81 Brambleleaf
A   82 Cherryleaf
A   84 Reliant
A   85 Faithful
A   86 Forceful
A   87 Favourite
A   88 Agile
A   89 Advice
A   90 Accord

Support Ships—contd.

A 91 Griper
A 92 Grinder
A 93 Dexterous
A 94 Director
A 95 Typhoon
A 96 Tidereach
A 97 Tideflow
A 98 Tidesurge
A 108 Triumph
A 111 Cyclone
A 122 Olwen
A 123 Olna
A 124 Olmeda
A 127 Torrent
A 128 Torrid
A 130 Gold Ranger
A 133 Hecla
A 134 Rame Head
A 135 Nordenfelt
A 137 Hecate
A 144 Hydra
(A 146 Protector)
A 154 Mermaid
(A 160 Fort Dunvegan)
A 163 Black Ranger
(A 164 Adamant)
A 169 Brown Ranger
A 185 Maidstone
(A 186 Fort Rosalie)
A 187 Defiance (Forth)
A 191 Berry Head
(A 194 Tyne)
A 200 Vidal
(A 204 Robert Dundas)
A 207 Wave Prince
A 212 Wave Ruler
A 218 Samsonia

Support Ships—contd.

A 219 Dewdale
A 221 Derwentdale
A 222 Spapool
A 223 Nimble
A 224 Spabrook
(A 225 Mull of Kintyre)
(A 229 Fort Duquesne)
(A 230 Fort Langley)
A 231 Reclaim
A 232 Kingarth
(A 236 Fort Charlotte)
A 240 Bustler
A 241 Robert Middleton
A 242 Wave Baron
A 257 Spaburn
A 259 St Margarets
A 260 Spalake
A 261 Eddyfirth
A 262 Hartland Point
A 264 Reward
A 265 Wave Chief
A 268 Green Rover
A 269 Grey Rover
A 270 Blue Rover
A 271 Gold Rover
A 280 Resurgent
A 281 Kinbrace
A 284 Rowanol
A 288 Sea Giant
A 289 Confiance
A 290 Confidant
A 293 Careful
(A 303 Dampier)
(A 307 Cook)
A 311 Owen
(A 316 Fort Sandusky)
A 317 Bulldog

Support Ships—contd.

A 319 Beagle
A 320 Fox
A 332 Caldy
A 333 Coll
A 334 Bern
A 335 Fawn
A 336 Lundy
A 338 Skomer
A 339 Lyness
A 340 Graemsay
A 342 Foulness
A 344 Stromness
A 345 Tarbatness
A 346 Switha
A 362 Dispenser
A 364 Whitehead
A 369 Empire Demon
A 372 Empire Fred
A 377 Maxim
A 378 Kinterbury
(A 387 Girdle Ness)
A 390 Samson
A 396 Frisky (Empire Rita)
A 397 Empire Rosa
A 399 Resolve (Empire Zona)
A 404 Bacchus
A 406 Hebe
A 480 Resource
A 482 Kinloss
A 486 Regent
A 489 Moorhen
A 491 Moorland
A 494 Salvalour
A 497 Salveda
A 499 Salvestor
A 500 Salvictor
A 503 Sea Salvor

Support Ships—contd.

A 505 Succour
A 506 Swin
A 507 Uplifter
A 508 Capable

(OCEAN MINESWEEPERS)

(M   46 Pluto) Barrow
(M 299 Rifleman) Barrow
(M 304 Waterwitch) Barrow

COASTAL MINESWEEPERS

(M 1101 Coniston)
M 1103 Alfriston (Kilmorey)
(M 1105 Amerton)
M 1109 Bickington
       (Killiecrankie)
M 1110 Bildeston
(M 1112 Boulston)
M 1113 Brereton
M 1114 Brinton
M 1115 Bronington
M 1116 Wilton
(M 1116 Burnaston)
(M 1117 Buttington)
(M 1118 Calton)
(M 1119 Carhampton)
(M 1120 Caunton)
(M 1122 Chilcompton)
(M 1123 Clarbeston)
M 1124 Crichton (St David)
M 1125 Cuxton
(M 1126 Dalswinton)
(M 1128 Derriton)
M 1130 Highburton

Coastal Minesweepers—contd.

M 1133 Bossington
(M 1135 Fenton)
M 1136 Fittleton (Curzon)
(M 1137 Flockton)
(M 1138 Floriston)
M 1140 Gavinton
M 1141 Glasserton
(M 1145 Dufton)
M 1146 Hodgeston (Venturer)
M 1147 Hubberston
(M 1149 Badminton)
(M 1150 Invermoriston)
M 1151 Iveston
M 1153 Kedleston
M 1154 Kellington
(M 1156 Kemerton)
M 1157 Kirkliston
M 1158 Laleston
(M 1159 Lanton)
(M 1160 Letterston)
(M 1161 Leverton)
(M 1162 Kildarton)
(M 1164 Maddiston)
M 1165 Maxton
M 1166 Nurton
M 1167 Repton (Clyde)
(M 1169 Penston)
(M 1170 Picton)
M 1173 Pollington (Mersey)
(M 1174 Puncheston)
(M 1175 Quainton)
(M 1177 Roddington)
(M 1179 Sefton)
M 1180 Shavington

Coastal Minesweepers Contd.

M 1181 Sheraton
M 1182 Shoulton
M 1187 Upton
M 1188 Walkerton
(M 1192 Wilkieston)
M 1194 Woolaston (Thames)
M 1195 Wotton
M 1198 Ashton
(M 1199 Belton)
(M 1200 Soberton)
(M 1202 Maryton)
(M 1203 Dartington)
M 1204 Stubbington
       (Montrose)
M 1205 Wiston
       (Northumbria)
(M 1206 Fiskerton)
M 1208 Lewiston
M 1209 Chawton
(M 1211 Houghton)
M 1216 Crofton (Solent)

INSHORE MINESWEEPERS

(M 2001 Dingley)
M 2002 Aveley
(M 2003 Brearley)
(M 2004 Brenchley)
(M 2005 Brinkley)
(M 2007 Broomley
       (Watchful))
(M 2008 Burley (Squirrel))
M 2009 Chailey
M 2010 Cradley (Isis)
M 2603 Arlingham PAS

Inshore Minesweepers—contd.

M 2611 Bottisham
       (ex-RAF 5000)
M 2614 Bucklesham TRV
M 2616 Chelsham (ex-RAF
       5001)
(M 2618 Cobham)
(M 2619 Darsham)
(M 2620 Davenham)
M 2621 Dittisham TRV
M 2622 Downham TRV
M 2626 Everingham PAS
M 2628 Flintham TRV
(M 2629 Damerham)
M 2630 Fritham TRV
M 2631 Glentham
M 2633 Halsham (RCT R G
       Masters, ex-RAF 5012)
M 2635 Haversham TRV
M 2636 Lasham TRV
(M 2637 Hovingham)
(M 2706 Ledsham)
(M 2708 Ludham)
(M 2713 Nettleham)
(M 2714 Ockham)
M 2716 Pagham RNXS
M 2717 Fordham DGV
M 2720 Powderham
       (Waterwitch)
(M 2722 Rackham)
M 2726 Shipham RNXS
(M 2727 Saxlingham)
(M 2728 Shrivenham)
M 2729 Sidlesham
       (Gerald Daniel)
       (Sussex Police)

Inshore Minesweepers—contd.

M 2733 Thakenham RNXS
M 2735 Tongham PAS
M. 2736 Tresham (RSNC
        Cardiff)
M 2737 Warmington DGV
(M 2778 Woldingham PAS)
M 2780 Woodlark
       (ex-Yaxham)
M 2781 Portisham RNXS
M 2783 Odiham RNXS
M 2784 Puttenham RNXS
M 2785 Birdham RNXS
(M 2787 Abbotsham)
(M 2788 Georgeham)
M 2790 Thatcham DGV
(M 2791 Sandringham) (Ferry)
(M 2792 Polsham
       (PLA Maplin))
M 2793 Thornham
       (Aberdeen University)

DGV
Converted to
Degaussing Vessels
PAS
Employed in the
Port Auxiliary Service
RNXS
Adapted for the
Royal Naval Auxiliary Service
TRV
Converted to
Torpedo Recovery Vessels

MOORING/SALVAGE/ BOOM VESSELS

P 190 Laymoor
P 191 Layburn
P 192 Mandarin
P 193 Pintail
P 194 Garganey
P 195 Goldeneye
(P 200 Barfoss)
P 201 Barbain
P 202 Barfoot
(P 214 Barbecue)
(P 216 Barglow)
(P 223 Moorpout)

Mooring/Salvage/Boom Vessels—contd.

P 232 Barmond
P 241 Barnard
(P 243 Barbican)
(P 244 Barfield)
P 254 Barrage
P 259 Barrington
(P 261 Bartizan)
(P 282 Barfoam)
P 284 Moorsman
P 294 Barfoil
P 297 Barnestone

FAST PATROL BOATS

P 271 Scimitar
P 274 Cutlass
P 275 Sabre
P 276 Tenacity
P 1011 Brave Borderer
P 1012 Brave Swordsman
(P 1048 Gay Charioteer)
(P 1101 Dark Adventurer)
(P 1112 Dark Hussar)
P 1114 Dark Gladiator
P 1115 Dark Hero
(P 1118 Dark Intruder)

COASTAL PATROL VESSELS

P 1007 Beachampton
(ex-M 1107)
P 1055 Monkton (ex-M 1155)
P 1089 Wasperton
(ex-M 1189)
P 1093 Wolverton
(ex-M 1193)
P 1096 Yarnton (ex-M 1196)

SEAWARD DEFENCE BOATS

P 3104 Beckford (Dee)
P 3113 Droxford
(P 3121 Kingsford)

A few of the ships listed above are on the sales list or have been earmarked for disposal, but their pennant numbers have been retained in this edition for reference and identification until they are actually broken up; and a few ships listed are not yet completed.

The pennant numbers of many submarines were changed on 1 May 1961, several 'A' class and 'T' class boats in the S 09 to S 27 range having been renumbered in the S 61 to S 74 range to enable all the post-war built conventional submarines to be numbered from S 01 to S 20 and onwards: Nuclear-powered fleet submarines were at the same time renumbered in a new S 101 series.

INDEX